AF020

MASSIMILIANO AFIERO

AXIS FORCES 20

The Axis Forces 020 - First edition March 2022 by Luca Cristini Editor for the brand Soldiershop
Cover & Art Design by soldiershop factory. ISBN code: 978-88-93278430

The Axis Forces **number 20 - March 2022**

Direction and editing: **Via San Giorgio, 11 – 80021 AFRAGOLA (NA) -ITALY**

Managing and Chief Editor: Massimiliano Afiero

Email: maxafiero@libero.it - **Website**: www.maxafiero.it

Contributors

Tomasz Borowski, Grégory Bouysse, Stefano Canavassi, Carlos Caballero Jurado, Rene Chavez, Gary Costello, Paolo Crippa, Carlo Cucut, Antonio Guerra, John B. Köser, Lars Larsen, Christophe Leguérandais, Eduardo M. Gil Martínez, Michael D. Miller, Peter Mooney, Péter Mujzer, Ken Niewiarowicz, Erik Norling, Raphael Riccio, Marc Rikmenspoel, Samcevich Andrei, Hugh Page Taylor, Charles Trang, Cesare Veronesi, Sergio Volpe

Editorial

Here is finally the first issue of our magazine of this troubled 2022. When it seemed that we were finally coming out of the health emergency created by Covid, the war in Ukraine came to complicate our lives. After almost eighty years of peace, Russia with the military invasion of Ukraine brought the war back to the old continent, causing serious damage to the economy and above all endangering the lives of entire populations. For years the situation in the Don basin was critical, explosive for some, due to the differences between the Ukrainians and the local Russian population, with numerous deaths on both sides. A war almost forgotten by everyone, limited, but which ultimately led to the current conflict. The Russian claims on those territories were perhaps legitimate, but the use of arms is always to be condemned, especially because it is causing death and destruction in a country that has always sought freedom and autonomy from Russia. Let's just hope that everything ends as soon as possible, that the weapons are silenced again in our old Europe and that a peaceful agreement is reached between the contenders! Let's now analyze the contents of this new issue of the magazine. Let's start with the history of the Wallonie assault brigade, from its formation to its use on the Ukrainian and Estonian fronts. Following that is the biography of a Latvian volunteer, Woldemars Veiss, one of the bravest officers, decorated with the Knight's Cross. We continue with the employment of the Totenkopf division in the Demyansk pocket, between January and March 1942. We conclude with a long, but hopefully interesting article by our friend Hugh Page Taylor on the recruitment centers for Italian SS volunteers, a great work of useful research for both historians and collectors. Always hoping to have met your interest in military history, I wish everyone happy reading and see you in the next issue.

Massimiliano Afiero

The publication of The Axis Forces deals exclusively with subjects of a historical military nature and is not intended to promote any type of political ideology either present or past, as it also does not seek to exalt any type of political regime of the past century or any form of racism.

Contents

LA BRIGADE D'ASSAUT
SS WALLONIE
vous parle...

The SS-Sturmbrigade Wallonien

By Massimiliano Afiero

Hauptmann Lucien Lippert with Leutnant Léon Degrelle, Spring 1943, in German uniform. Note the oval with the Edelweiss, on the right sleeve of the uniform of Lippert, as a sign of recognition for the employment of the Walloon Legion with the *97.Jäger Division* in the Caucasus campaign (U.S. NARA).

Walloon officers at Pieske camp with Himmler: from the left, Jean Vermeire, Himmler and Lucien Lippert (DC).

In the autumn of 1942, after meeting *SS-Brigdf.* Felix Steiner, commander of the SS *Wiking* division, during the fighting in the Caucasus, Degrelle had specifically asked General Rupp to subordinate *Wallonie* to the *Wiking*, but without the authorization of the German high command, nothing could be done. In mid-December 1942, taking advantage of the first leave granted to his legionaries,

Degrelle went to Paris for a new campaign of enlistments and to negotiate with the German authorities the release of the Belgian prisoners still locked up in German concentration camps. Unable to find any agreement, the Rexist leader decided to turn to the *Waffen-SS*, thanks to the support of the correspondent of the Pays Réel newspaper, the historian Léon Van Huffel, who introduced him to the high command of the SS.

Walloons volunteers with the new Waffen-SS uniforms during training, Summer 1943. Note that one volunteer wear on the uniform the Walloon Rexist badge also known as the Blood Order, instituted in 1941 (U.S. NARA).

The Walloon Rexist Honor badge, Silver Class, was instituted in 1941.

And so, in January 1943, a new recruitment campaign was launched for the Walloon unit, this time with the help of the SS propaganda service. Hundreds of new volunteers from all social classes came to the enlistmen centers. In addition to a good number of ex-miners and workers, there were many officers and soldiers of the old Belgian army, young people of the nobility, of the best Belgian bourgeoisie, children of diplomats, officials and industrialists. On June 1, 1943, through the direct intercession of Gottlob Berger, head of the *SS-Hauptamt*, the Walloon legion with its two thousand men, was officially incorporated into the *Waffen-SS*, becoming the *SS-Freiwilligen-Brigade 'Wallonien'*[1]. The results achieved by the Legion on the Eastern front had greatly impressed *Reichsführer-SS* Heinrich Himmler. The new Brigade was transferred to the Pieske camp near Meseritz. It included survivors of the Legion, joined by former soldiers of the Belgian army and more than 400 new recruits. This brought he unit up to a strength of more than two thousand men.

Members of the Formations de Combat with Walloon volunteers, during the formation of the Brigade, summer 1943 (U.S. NARA).

The new arm shield produced for the Brigade *Wallonien* by the Germans, the national colors and the word Wallonie.

The command of the unit was assigned to *SS-Stubaf.* Lucien Lippert. The Brigade was shortly after moved to the Wildflecken camp in the Rhön region. On July 3, 1943, the unit was renamed *SS-Sturmbrigade 'Wallonien'*, then a new motorized assault brigade of the *Waffen-SS*. The new brigade included three rifle companies, a heavy company, a motorcycle platoon, a pioneer platoon, a transportation company, a depot company, a general staff and logistic units. The training was completed in October 1943. With the new SS uniform, for the Walloon volunteers a new arm shield was produced by the Germans, with a simpler, less elaborate, always with the national colors and the word *Wallonie*. However, most of the volunteers continued to use the Legion's arm shield.

Transfer to Ukraine

At the beginning of November 1943, the Brigade was transferred in Ukraine and on November 11, it became subordinate to the *Wiking* division, which was fighting on the Dnieper front, in the area north of Cherkassy. The convoys of the *Sturmbrigade* passed through Lemberg, Jassy and Kisinev. Walloon volunteers landed at Korsun station on the night of November 19-20. They were reinforced by a battery of assault guns from the *SS-Polizei-Division*, including *StuG.III* and under the orders of *SS-Hstuf.* Planitzer.

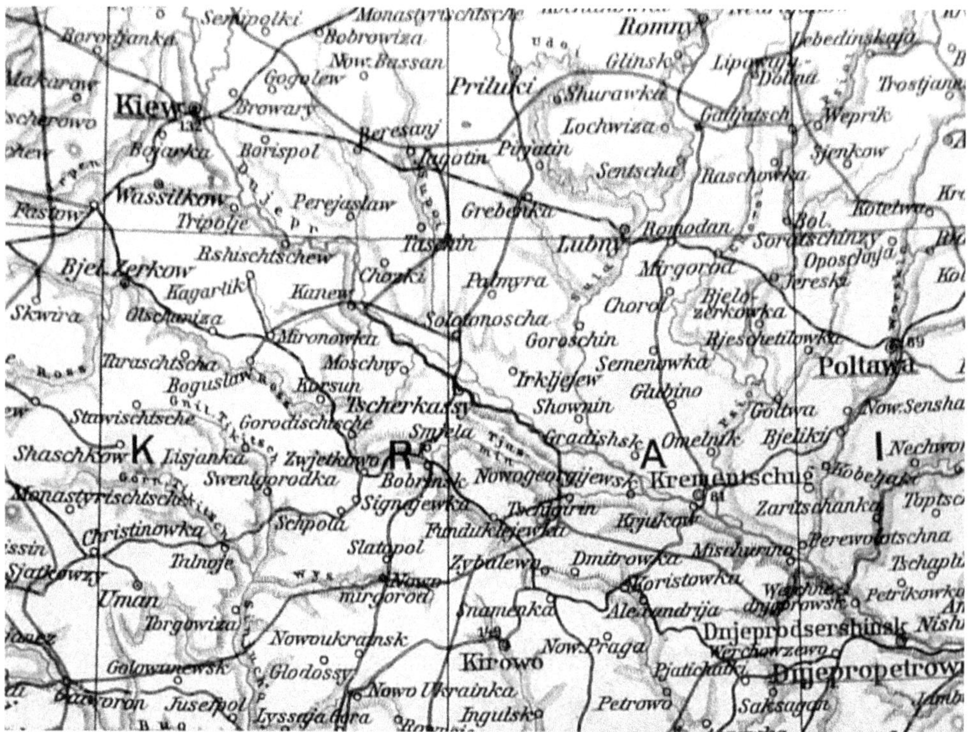

The area where was transferred the Walloon Brigade, at southeast of Kiev.

Walloon volunteers on the Ukrainian front, Autumn 1943.

On November 26, *SS-Gruf.* Herbert-Otto Gille, commander of the *Wiking* division since 1 May 1943, located the units of the *'Wallonie'* along the course of the Olschanka river. The *2.Kompanie* of *SS-Ostuf.* Henri Derricks, was kept in reserve in Smela. The Olschanka sector seemed fairly peaceful, but in reality the whole region was teeming with partisans. Commander Lippert then organized patrols to conduct reconnaissance across the river to maintain control of the terrain. One of these patrols, led by *SS-Ostuf.* Hubert van Eyser, on December 13, fell into an ambush in the Sakaloroskaja area: almost all the entire patrol ended up annihilated by enemy fire. Only six survivors, all injured, managed to return to the friendly lines.

A 8,1 cm mortar (*m.Gr.W.34*) of the *Wallonien* on the Ukrainian front, Autumn 1943.

Walloon sentry, Autumn 1943.

The first real fight, however, did not take place until December 22, in Yrdin, where the *3.Kompanie* under the orders of Léon Degrelle, was engaged in hard defensive fighting. During the month of December, the front defended by the Walloon volunteers was shortened again, going from twenty to seven kilometers, due to the reduced strength of the brigade. Opposite the positions of the Walloons was the Cherkassy forest. Their lines extended from Losowok to Starosselje. On January 4, 1944, to try to ease the strong enemy pressure, the brigade launched an attack on the village of Sakrewka, an attack that ended in complete success. This lifted the Walloons' morale after bad news about an imminent encirclement of German forces in the Korsun-Cherkassy region. The brigade remained in defense of the sector of Mochny, only to be taken over four days later by the

A Walloon *Untersturmführer* on the Ukrainian front, Autumn 1943 (U.S. NARA).

January 1944: a group of Walloon volunteers during a pause in the Korsun pocket (U.S. NARA).

III./Westland. On January 15, 1944, Walloon volunteers were engaged in the Teclino forest, against a strong concentration of partisans supported by regular Soviet troops. The battle was fierce. Among the Soviets there were many women with shaved heads who fought like lionesses. The Walloons lost two hundred men in a few minutes. Between January 15-18, however, the brigade managed to destroy 600 enemy bunkers. But the fighting did not stop, due to the strong obstinacy of the Soviet units. The Walloons were later grouped in Beloserje, where they were reviewed by *SS-Gruf.* Gille and on the occasion numerous awards were presented to the Walloon volunteers.

The Korsun pocket

On January 28, the threat of encirclement became a reality: two German army corps, with six divisions and the *SS-Sturmbrigade Wallonie*, were surrounded around Korsun. The Walloons found themselves at the eastern end of the pocket. On February 2, at 8:00 am, the Soviets attacked in strength between Losowok and the Dnieper River. The few Walloons defending the sector were overwhelmed and Losowok's position was lost. The *2.Kompanie* immediately launched a counterattack with the support of *Wiking* panzers, managing to recapture the village of Losowok after a furious hand-to-hand fight. But it was all in vain, since the German command immediately afterwards decided to evacuate the sector. The next day, the brigade regrouped in Beloserje. His new defensive front extended at that time for about thirty kilometers, from

Starosselje to Derenkowez. To defend it, there were only three hundred grenadiers completely tried by previous fighting, practically one man every one hundred meters. In the meantime, numerous Soviet penetrations had already taken place.

SS-Hauptsturmführer **Léon Degrelle with his men from** ***SS-Sturmbrigade Wallonien*** **in the Cherkassy/Korsun Pocket in early 1944 (U.S. NARA).**

Léon Degrelle and some of the survivors of the Walloon ***Sturmbrigade*** **after escaping the Cherkassy/Korsun Pocket.**

Most of the roads, transformed into immense quagmires due to a sharp thaw, were immediately cut off from the Soviet units. The Brigade was working hard to reach its new positions due to the disastrous state of the roads, congested by the huge traffic of military vehicles but also by the thousands of Ukrainian civilians who had decided to follow the German units in their retreat. On February 5, the Walloons settled in the trenches dug in the previous months by Ukrainian workers. But even this new defensive line could not hold for long. In fact, as early as February 6, the Soviets attacked again. Completely overwhelmed, the volunteers of the

Waffen-SS were now fighting only to save their skin. After furious fighting, the Walloon SS units managed to fall back in good order in the late afternoon. Some men were still stationed between Derenkowez and Starosselje. For the next two days, fighting continued. The village of Skiti was lost and then reconquered after a particularly bloody battle: Walloons and Soviets fought like wild beasts, clashing with every type of weapon in furious melee of combat. On February 9, with the pocket slowly moving west, the Walloon volunteers received orders to cover the retreat of the other German units that were still surrounded, continuing to be engaged in hard rearguard fighting. More than a hundred vehicles from the Walloon Brigade were destroyed by Soviet tanks during the retreat. The Derenkowez position was abandoned on February 11: the Walloons, in a strength ratio of one to ten, had managed to hold the location despite the enormous numerical superiority of the Soviets. On February 13, the Brigade arrived in Novo Buda, where the unit would entrench itself in a defensive position.

February 20, 1944: *SS-Gruf.* Gille, General Lieb and Léon Degrelle, waiting to be received by the *Führer* to receive respectively the Swords, the Oak Leaves and the Knight's Cross (*Charles Trang*).

All Soviet attacks were repelled. The next day, during a new Soviet attack, *SS-Stubaf.* Lippert was killed near his command post following a grenade explosion. *SS-Hstuf.* Léon Degrelle replaced him at the command of the SS Brigade and moving to the most threatened points, he managed to improve the men's morale. On February 16, German forces inside the pocket attempted a desperate breakout maneuver. With a forced march to the west, a breach was opened, but paying a very high price: only 632 Walloons managed to finally cross the Gniloj Tikitsch river and thus reached the lines held by the German troops of the *III.Pz.Korps.*

Triumphal parade in Belgium

The heroism shown by Walloon volunteers during the battle of Korsun/Cherkassy was exploited by German propaganda: after receiving the Knight's Cross from from Hitler in person, Léon Degrelle gave a speech at the Palais de Chaillot in Paris in front of an audience of about ten thousand people. After, he joined his men in Wlodawa, Poland.

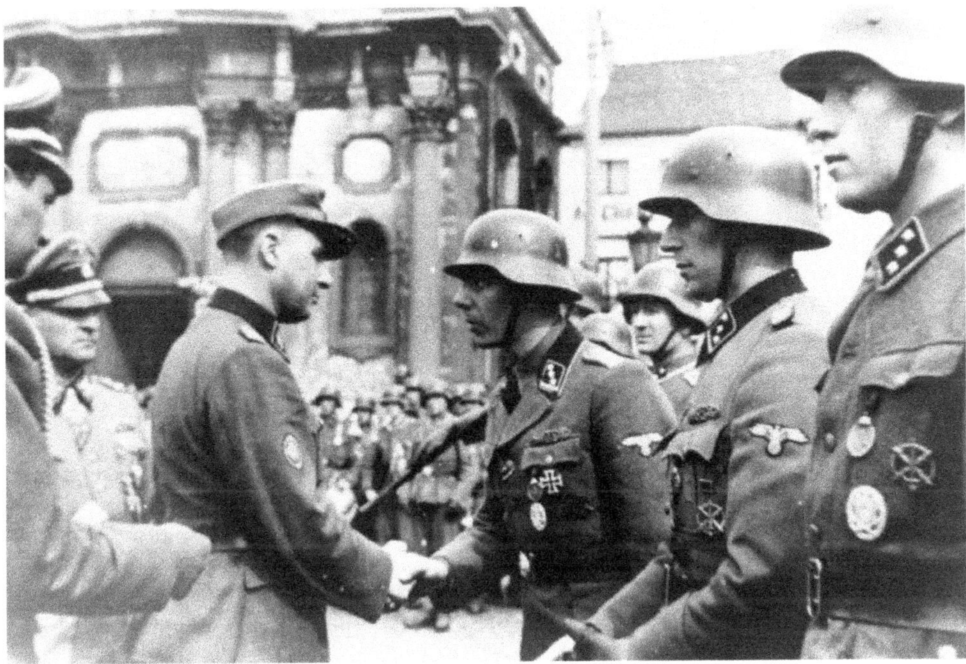

Léon Degrelle (center-left) awarding medals to members of the Walloon SS, Charleroi, April 1,1944. From the left, Roger Wastiau, Josef Dietrich, Léon Degrelle, Marcel Lamproye, Pascal Bovy, Marcel Bonniver and Jean-Marie Lantier.

Walloon Brigade parade in Brussels, April 1944, with Half-tracks of *12.SS-Panzerdivision 'Hitlerjugend'*.

Again for propaganda reasons, it was decided that Walloon volunteers would participate in a large parade to put an end to false rumors spread by Soviet propaganda: in fact, Stavka had pompously announced that all German units, including the *Wiking* division and the Brigade *Wallonien,* surrounded in the Cherkassy-Korsun pocket, had been completely annihilated. The Brigade then reached Wildflecken camp before reaching Beverloo, Belgium, where the unit was to be put back on its feet. The famous training camp of the Belgian army at that time mainly housed the units of the *12.SS-Panzerdivision 'Hitlerjugend'*. The Division had to relinquish its vehicles temporarily to the Walloon

Brigade. The first parade took place in Charleroi, in the presence of important German personalities. On this occasion, 75 Walloon volunteers were decorated with the Iron Cross.

Walloon Brigade parade in Brussels, Degrelle's children are with him.

Walloon volunteer (NARA).

The Brigade later reached Brussels, where it triumphantly paraded through the streets of the city. The Walloons were transferred a few days later back to Wildflecken camp, where the unit was reorganized with the following order of battle:

5.SS-Freiwilligen-Sturmbrigade 'Wallonien'
- *Brigade Stab*
- *I.Bataillon (1.-4.Kp.)*
- *II.Bataillon (5.-8.Kp.)*
- *Infanterie-Geschütz-Kompanie*
- *Panzerjäger-Kompanie*
- *leichte Flak-Batterie*
- *schwere Flak-Batterie*
- *Feldersatz-Kompanie*
- *Versorgungs-Kompanie*

Walloon volunteers and Léon Degrelle on the Estonian Front, Summer 1944 (U.S. NARA).

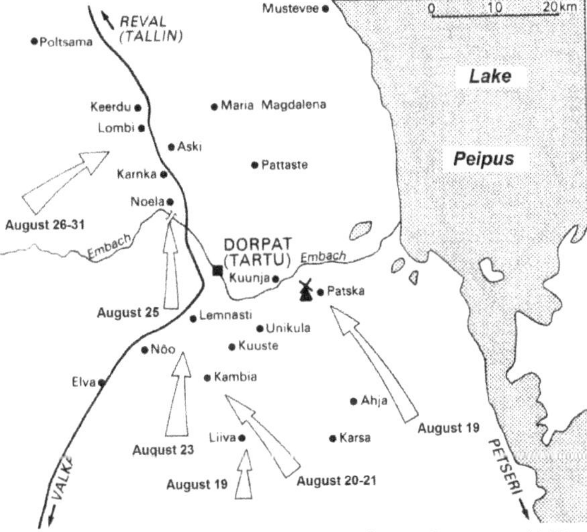

Soviet offensive on the Estonian front, Summer 1944.

From the left, *SS-Brigdf.* Wagner and Léon Degrelle.

In June 30, 1944, the unit included 53 officers, 232 non-commissioned officers and 903 soldiers, for a total of 1,188 men. A number very far from the theoretical force for an SS motorized brigade.

On the Estonian Front

At the end of July, while Degrelle was forbidden to return to the front line, again for propaganda reasons, one of the battalions of the brigade was sent, without consulting the Rexist leader, to the Estonian front. Degrelle then decided to reach the Baltic coast on his own initiative. Here, he managed to convince *SS-Brigf.* Jürgen Wagner, commander of the SS *Nederland* Brigade, to leave his *Kampfgruppe* in reserve, in order to continue training the new recruits. And so, *Kampfgruppe Degrelle*, including the *I. Bataillon* and the *Pz.Jg.-Kompanie* for a total of about five hundred men, was deployed on the coast of the Gulf of Finland, in the rear of the *Tannenberg-Stellung,* where the *III.SS-Pz.Korps* was fighting strenuously. In mid-August, south of Lake Peipus, the German defensive front was overwhelmed under strong Soviet pressure. The Narwa front was in danger of being circumvented. The *III.SS-Pz.Korps* then organized a *Kampfgruppe,* under the orders of *SS-Brigdf.* Wagner, to try to stop the Soviet advance in southern Estonia. The Walloon volunteers were attached to *Kampfgruppe Wagner,* which anchored its defense around Tartu.

Léon Degrelle takes a break at a fountain during the fighting in Estonia, Summer 1944 (U.S. NARA).

Walloon soldiers on the Estonian front.

On August 16, the Walloon units stood in a defensive position alongside the *11.Infanterie-Division*. On the 19th, they came into contact with major Soviet forces in Patska and on the windmill hill. Supported by four panzers, the Walloons held their positions, but at the same time, the Soviets overwhelmed the German-Estonian units, which fell back into great disorder. Between 21 and 22 August, the Walloons defended Kambia's position from repeated Soviet attacks. On August 23, the Noo position fell into the hands of the Soviets. The Kambia position was so threatened, as were the roads leading to Tartu. *SS-Untersturmfiihrer* Léon Gillis established an anti-tank barrier on this road, repelling enemy assaults and inflicting heavy casualties on the Soviets. On August 24, the German General Staff ordered the Walloons to defend the Kambia position at any cost. However, despite the support of Hans Rudel's *Stukas*, this order proved difficult to execute. Degrelle then retreated with his men to the northwest, south of the Embach River. As soon as night fell, he launched a counterattack, but without success. On August 25, the battle for Tartu began. The Walloon volunteers were engaged in Noëla, about twenty kilometers south-west of the university city. Fierce fighting followed which lasted for several days, with the Walloons defending their positions strenuously, engaging all available men on the front lines: secretaries, warehouse workers, drivers, lightly wounded.

Walloon volunteers.

Also in Parma, Lombi and Keerow, they fought fanatically and were mentioned three times in the official bullettin of the *III.SS-Pz.Korps*. On August 30, determined to end the game, the Soviets engaged major forces against the positions held by Degrelle's men, launching an attack every thirty minutes. But they failed to pass. This defensive success however cost the Walloons dearly: of the 260 Walloon volunteers present at the beginning of August 30, only 32 were still standing at the end of the day. The battalion no longer had any combat value and was withdrawn from the front. All the survivors were decorated with the Iron Cross, while Léon Degrelle added the Oak Leaves to his Knight's Cross. On September 20, 1944, the *SS-FHA* decided to transform the *'Wallonien'* into a new SS division, the *28.SS-Freiwilligen-Grenadier-Division 'Wallonien'*, using as personnel all the men capable of carrying a weapon among the mass of refugees who had fled after the allied invasion of Belgium.

Léon Degrelle receive the Oak Leaves from the *Führer*, at presence of Felix Steiner.

Note

(1) Strangely, although not of Germanic race, Walloon volunteers were assigned grades with the prefix *'SS'*, normally reserved for Germanic volunteers, instead of the prefix *'Waffen'*.

Bibliography

M. Afiero, "*Belgian Waffen-SS Legion & Brigade 1941–44*", Osprey Publishing

Waffen-Standartenführer der SS Woldermars Veiss

by Peter Mooney

Waffen-Standartenführer der SS **Woldermars Veiss.**

Veiss awarding Latvian legionnaires, Volkhov 1943.

Born in Riga, Latvia, his military career started on Christmas Day 1918 with the Latvian Army. By late-May 1919 he had obtained Officer rank, which then progressed further to 1st Lieutenant during February 1920. He was promoted to Captain in 1935 (after spending 3 years at the Riga war academy) and then in 1937 was holding Lieutenant-Colonel rank. He served in Finland and Estonia in 1939. From June 1941, he was actively fighting Partisans with the Latvian Schutzmannschaft units, under the overall control and command of the Germans.

When the Latvian units were being raised for the SS in April 1943, Veiss transferred with his Latvian Army rank and became a *Waffen-Obersturmbannführer der SS,* which quickly changed to *Waffen-Standartenführer der SS* in August. He was given command of the *1. Lettisches SS-Freiwilligen Regiment*. He had been fighting on the Wolchow front near Leningrad since early May 1943. The award of the Second Class Iron Cross came on the 20th of July, with the First Class Iron Cross being awarded in September. On the 27th of January 1944, Hinrich Schuldt, Commander of the *2. Lettisches SS-Freiwilligen*

Brigade, penned a recommendation for the award of Veiss' Knight's Cross, reading as follows: 'SS-Standartenführer *Veiss, as the leader of* Kampfgruppe Veiss, *has been fighting the enemy in the most difficult manner and prevented them from taking the place of Nekoschowo, following exceptional defense by his troops at Podporesje. Through daring advances along the railway line and railroad station at Tatino, moving southwards, he broke through enemy attacks and inflicted severe destruction on them.*

***Waffen-Ostubaf.* Veiss awarding Latvian legionnaires, Volkhov, Summer 1943.**

***Waffen-Ostubaf.* Woldermars Veiss.**

After days of fighting in the swamps and forests, he attacked Dolgowo using his own initiative. He alsoheld Tatino for several days and therefore held the advance of strong hostile groups, which was moving against the open left flank of KG "General Speth", *significantly weakening and delaying them. By these attacks, done under his robust personal leadership, the enemy suffered heavy losses.*

These battle successes of the Latvian Brigade were crucial for the heavy defensive battles of the XXXVIII. Army Korps. *Influenced by his outstanding attitude, personal bravery and hard determination, all obstacles have been overcome; he had cleverly moved his troops forward.* SS-Standartenführer *leads the Brigade during this time. He has maintained the highest efforts in defence and attack in the final days. The Commander in Chief has verbally spoken of his appreciation, through the Commanding General, and personally in writing. I recommend that* SS-Standartenführer *Veiss, in agreement with the warmest support from the* XXXVIII. Army Korps, *is awarded the Knight's Cross of the Iron Cross.'*

***Waffen-Ostubaf.* Woldermars Veiss (right) 2nd in command for *2. Lettische SS-Freiwilligen Brigade* which became *19. Waffen Grenadier Division der SS (lettische Nr 2)* in January 1944, briefs his troops in September 1943.**

***Waffen-Ostubaf.* Woldemars Veiss**

This proposal was backed up with a letter written on the 4th of February by General Herzog, the Commander of the *XXXVIII. Army Korps*. That letter highlighted Veiss and the bravery displayed by the men under his command. It also mentions the tenacity of the Latvians, the fact that Veiss was always at the head of his men and specifically points Veiss out as an example of a great fighter. Himmler supported the Schuldt recommendation with a short addendum to the typed version of the recommendations, dated the 8th of February. This multi-level suggestion was approved the following day. The approval gave the Latvian SS units their first Knight's Cross; it would be one of two awarded in this timeframe (but not the first Latvian-born Waffen-SS Knight's Cross holder, as Berndt Lubich von Milovan preceded him by almost four months and Heinrich Sonne by two months).

***SS-Standartenführer* Woldemars Veiss.**

Veiss funeral in Riga.

Veiss funeral in Riga: the coffin on the back of a *Marder III*.

When proposed, the unit was titled the *2. (Lettisches) SS-Freiwilligen Brigade*, but by the time of the approval, they had been renamed the *19. Waffen-Grenadier-Division der SS (Lettisches Nr. 2)*, so it is that unit that we will 'count' this award under. Veiss himself was given command of *Waffen-Grenadier Regiment der SS 42* within the *19. Waffen-Grenadier-Division der SS (Lettisches Nr. 2)* during March 1944. Back at the front, Veiss was heavily wounded by grenade shrapnel on the 7th of April. He was evacuated by air to Riga, but died on the 17th of April 1944 due to the severity of the wounds. He received a full military burial, with his coffin being transported on the back of a *Marder III* self-propelled anti-tank gun.

Bibliography

Peter Mooney, "*Waffen-SS Knights and their Battles*", Schiffer Military History

The SS-Totenkopf-Division in the Demjansk pocket

by Massimiliano Afiero

SS-Gruppenführer **Theodor Eicke.**

Totenkopf **Artillery observers, January 1942.**

In early December 1941, the temperature on the Eastern Front continued to fall precipitously, reaching thirty below (Celsius). Due to the cold, weapons began to jam and vehicle motors froze up, delaying the arrival of supplies. The Soviets took advantage of that to launch a general offensive, from the Baltic Sea to the Black Sea. The Germans retreated everywhere, abandoning tanks, heavy weapons and vehicles along the way. At that time the offensive did not involve the Valdai area, which stayed fairly quiet. During that same period, to continue to make reconnaissance missions in enemy territory, the *Totenkopf* headquarters ordered that a ski company be formed, led by *SS-Ostuf.* Eduard Weber. On December 18, Adolf Hitler ordered his troops in Russia to hold the positions they had reached at all costs and not to retreat; that order, as dramatic as it was and calling for sacrifice, saved the German army from a complete rout. On December 26, Theodor Eicke was awarded the Knight's Cross for the valor shown by his men during the defensive fighting of the previous autumn.

The Soviet winter counteroffensive

During the night between January 7-8, 1942, the Soviets launched a massive offensive against the right wing of *Heeresgruppe "Nord"*: three armies were able to break through the German front, between lakes Ilmen and Seliger, while further to the south the Soviet 3rd Shock

Army broke through the *16.Armee* lines. Within a few hours, the Soviets had wiped out the *290.Inf.Div.*, deployed to the right of *Totenkopf* and penetrated for about thirty kilometers behind *X.Armee-Korps* lines. On January 9, the Soviet 11th Army reached Staraya Russa and then turned to the south. At the same time, the Soviet 1st Shock Army, attacking west of Lake Seliger, advanced along the Lowat to establish contact with the 11th Army, thus threatening to surround the entire *16.Armee*.

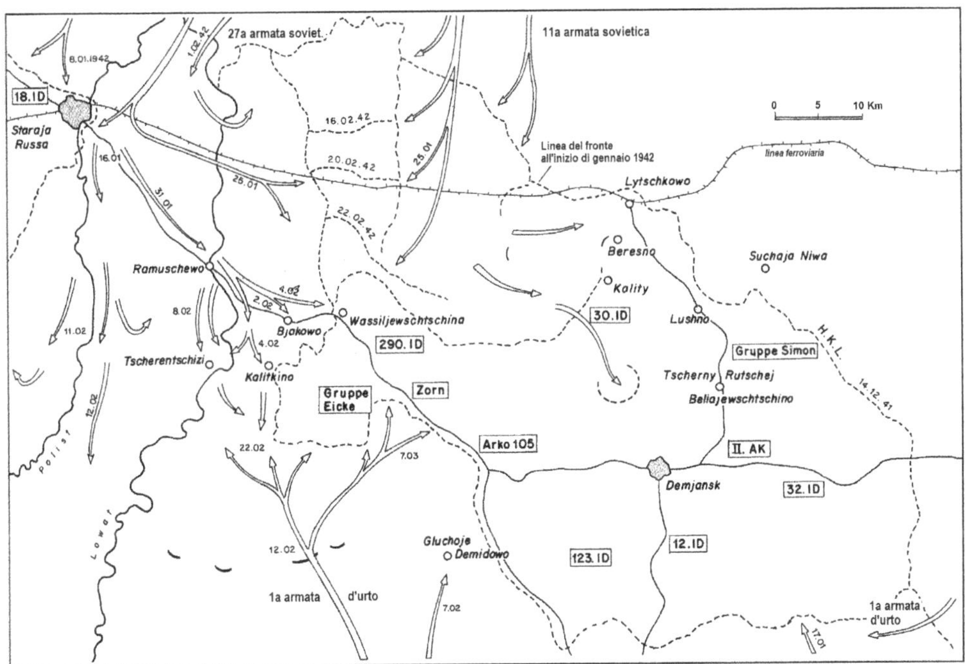

The axes of the Soviet winter offensive in the *II.Armee-Korps* sector, with dates.

***Totenkopf* soldiers in the Demjansk sector.**

Realizing the danger, *16.Armee* ordered the *Totenkopf* to form *Kampfgruppen* to send immediately to the Staraya Russa sector. That city was the supply base for *16.Armee*: there were warehouses full of food and ammunition, repair shops and hospitals there. The Staraya Russa – Ramuschewo – Kobylkino –Wassilijewschtschina - Demjansk road, through which all of the supplies for *II.Armee-Korps* and *X.Armee-Korps* passed, was directly threatened by the northern arm of the Soviet offensive. The *16.Armee* headquarters early on identified the Soviet axis of attack. Considering that at that moment the Valdai region was not directly threatened by the enemy's attack, the

Totenkopf was ordered to withdraw many of its units from its front lines in order to shift them to more threatened points of the front. The *Totenkopf* chose to send its reconnaissance group to the Staraya Russa area, whose command in the meantime had been assumed by *SS-Stubaf.* Adolf Kurtz. However, the *Totenkopf* recon troops were stopped along the way so that they could be attached to the *18.Inf.Div.(mot.)* which at that time was in dire straits in the Podborowje area.

A *Totenkopf* battery equipped with the 150 mm *sIG33* (*U.S. National Archives*).

***Totenkopf* soldiers in winter dress.**

After having been engaged along the western shores of Lake Ilmen, *18.Infanterie-Division* had been ordered to move towards Staraya Russa. During the march, strong Soviet units attacked the flanks of the German division, forcing it to withdraw to the Polist River; in the end, only *Inf.Regiment 51* was able to reach that city.

The fight for Staraya Russa

Eicke received a peremptory order from the corps headquarters: *"...You will send five battalions to Staraya Russa. It is important to hold this important communications hub at all costs"*. On January 8, the following *Totenkopf* combat groups were sent towards Staraya Russa:

-SS-Artillerie-Gruppe "Stange": SS-Hstuf. Stange
Stab I.SS-T.Art.-Rgt.
4./SS-T.Art.Rgt.
10./SS-T.Art.Rgt.

A *Totenkopf* ski trooper, January 1942.

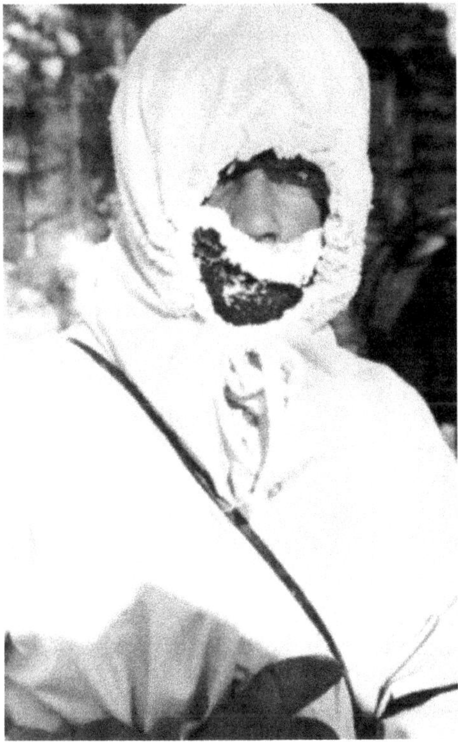

A *Totenkopf* soldier, January 1942.

-SS-Kampfgruppe "Ullrich": SS-Hstuf. Ullrich
Stab SS-T.Pi.-Btl.
2./SS-T.Pi.-Btl.
3./SS-T.Pi.-Btl.

-SS-Kampfgruppe "Eichert": SS-Ostuf. Eichert
1./SS-T.Kradsch.-Btl.
IG-Zug "Dunkmann"

-SS-Kmpf. "Bochmann": SS-Hstuf. Bochmann
Stab SS-T.Pz.Jg.-Abt.

-SS-Kmpf. "Wedenig": SS-Ostuf. Wedenig
10./SS-Tot.Inf.Rgt.1
Elements of 12./SS-Tot.Inf.Rgt.1

-SS-Kampfgruppe "Becker": SS-Ostubaf. Becker
Stab SS-Tot.Inf.Rgt.3

Elem. *SS-T.StuG.-Bttr.: SS-Ostuf. Meierdress*

Once they had arrived in Staraya Russa, all of these *Kampfgruppen* were attached to *18.Infanterie-Division* commanded by *Generalleutnant* Werner von Erdmannsdorff. The headquarters of *SS-Tot.Inf.Rgt.3* assumed responsibility for the northern sector of the defensive front. The *10.Bttr./SS-Tot.Art.-Rgt.*, commanded by *SS-Ostuf.* Konrath, sited its guns close to the airport. As soon as the guns had been been emplaced, the SS gunners were attacked by Soviet tanks and infanry who had in the meantime crossed the Polist River. The SS gunners fired feverishly against the enemy until the attackers fell back. Soon after, the Soviets attacked again and continued attacking throughout the night; in the morning, the exhausted SS gunners counted hundreds of enemy dead in front of their positions. On January 9, 1942, the situation became even more difficult for the Germans; it now seemed impossible to fill the breach between Staraya Russa and the positions held by *290.Inf.Div.* Numerous Soviet formations worked their way closer to the Staraya Russa-Demjansk road and pushed back units of *18.Inf.Div.(mot.)*. The *SS-T.Aufkl.-Abt.* was attacked right in the middle of a snow storm by a battalion of Soviet ski troops. The SS recon troops had to withdraw to Mednikowa, where they linked up with *SS-Kampfgruppe Becker*. Meanwhile, Staraya Russa was taken under fire by Soviet artillery, which shelled it without letup.

A *Totenkopf* scout patrol, January 1942.

Soviet infantry attacking, January 1942.

An *MG 34* defending a *Totenkopf* position (NA).

A *Totenkopf* defensive position with a medium mortar.

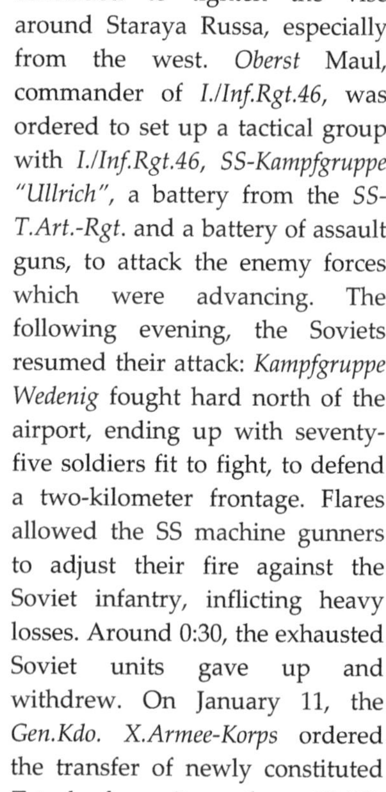

On January 10, the Soviet units continued to tighten the vise around Staraya Russa, especially from the west. *Oberst* Maul, commander of *I./Inf.Rgt.46*, was ordered to set up a tactical group with *I./Inf.Rgt.46, SS-Kampfgruppe "Ullrich"*, a battery from the *SS-T.Art.-Rgt.* and a battery of assault guns, to attack the enemy forces which were advancing. The following evening, the Soviets resumed their attack: *Kampfgruppe Wedenig* fought hard north of the airport, ending up with seventy-five soldiers fit to fight, to defend a two-kilometer frontage. Flares allowed the SS machine gunners to adjust their fire against the Soviet infantry, inflicting heavy losses. Around 0:30, the exhausted Soviet units gave up and withdrew. On January 11, the *Gen.Kdo. X.Armee-Korps* ordered the transfer of newly constituted *Totenkopf* units, the *III./SS-*

Tot.Inf.Rgt.3 and the *9.Bttr./SS-Tot.Art.-Rgt.*, units which were used to form *Kampgruppe Moder* commanded by *SS-Stubaf.* Moder, to the *290.Inf.Div.* in order to reinforce the southern flank of *16.Armee*. During the night between January 11-12, the Soviets attempted to take Mednikowa, but were driven off by machine gun fire and direct fire by *4.Bttr./SS-T.Art.-Rgt.* The Soviets mounted a fresh attack against *Kampfruppe Wedenig*, which was repulsed with heavy enemy losses. The assault guns under *SS-Ostuf.* Erwin Meierdress were employed throughout the day along the Korostyn road.

German *StuG.III* assault guns on the Demjansk front, January 1942.

***SS-Ostuf.* Erwin Meierdress.**

During the fighting, *SS-Ostuf.* Meierdress was himself seriously wounded. The *SS-Tot.Pi.-Btl.* reached Staraya Russa and occupied defensive positions to the east of the city. The critical situation southeast of that spot led the headquarters of *18.Infanterie-Division* to throw Gruppe Maul into a counterattack towards the forest known as *"the forest of the Laplanders"*. *SS-Bataillon "Bochmann"* managed to reach the position, but at the same time, Soviet troops supported by about twenty tanks attacked the flanks. The SS troops withdrew to Lipowizy, where a total of fourteen Soviet tanks were destroyed at close range with hand grenades and magnetic mines. In the afternoon, *X.Armee-Korps* again asked for the intervention of the *Totenkopf* to free forces from the

Valdai front so that they could be committed to the Staraya Russa sector. On January 13, 1942, there were new attacks against Staraya Russa: northwest of the position, the Soviets cut the Schimsk road. *SS-Kampfgruppe Becker* was then ordered to see to the defense of part of the western side of Staraya Russa.

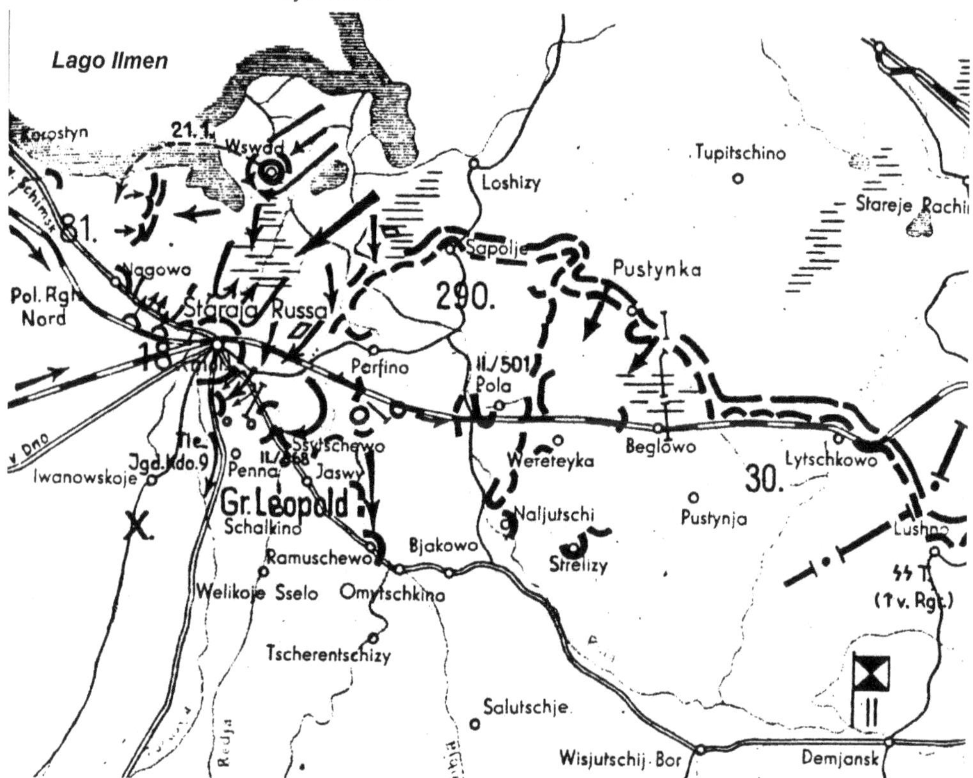

The situation in the Staraya Russa area between January 1-31, 1942. The black arrows indicate Soviet attacks against German positions.

A *Totenkopf* 20 mm *Flak* gun on the Valdai front.

To that end, a *Luftwaffe* Feldregiment and alert units were attached to it. At the same time, in the area to the east of Staraya Russa, *Kampfgruppe Ullrich* was battered by Soviet artillery fire. During the following days all of the Soviet attacks against Staraya Russa were driven off and the Schimsk road came under German control again. On January 15, the *Totenkopf* passed under the control of *II.A-K.* Almost half of its infantry units and a large part of its artillery had been detached in support of *290.Inf.Div.* or was engaged on the Staraya Russa front. In the space of a week, the overall situation had worsened significantly for the Germans.

***Totenkopf* soldiers during a transfer march.**

German infantry and tanks on the Demjansk front.

***Totenkopf* soldiers moving in the attack.**

To the south there was an eighty kilometer wide gap between *16.Armee* and *9.Armee*, while the Soviet 1st Shock Army was advancing on Kholm. Called on to defend a ninety kilometer front, the *123.Inf.Div.* proved incapable of holding its positions. The remnants of *32.Inf.Div.* and of the *123.Inf.Div.* established a new defensive front that was fully a hundred and ninety kilometers long. The Soviets exploited the breach to push to the west, using brigades of ski troops supported by tanks and thus threatening the *II.Armee-Korps* rear area. To the north of Staraya Russa the Soviets were able to cut the railway line to Schimsk. Southeast of the city, they headed towards the Lovat, thus surrounding *II.Armee-Korps* and *X.Armee-Korps*.

To stabilize the front at Molwotizy, *II.Armee-Korps* pulled new units from *Totenkopf* from the Valdai front. A mixed battalion, commanded by *SS-Stubaf.* Otto Kron, commander of the *SS-Totenkopf-Flak-Abteilung*, was thus thrown into the battle along with the engineers of *16.(Pi.)Kp./SS-Tot.Inf.Rgt.1.* These two *Totenkopf* units managed to repel all of the Soviet attacks until the middle of April. The permanent threat that hung over the *II.Armee-Korps* right flank forced it to send additional forces to Staraya Russa and Demjansk. The *X.Armee-Korps* also sent units to the south; a *Totenkopf* motorcycle company was sent to Nikolino. On January 20, forced by Hitler's orders to hold its positions, the *II.Armee-Korps* found itself completely cut off in the Demjansk area, after the Soviet 27th Army had cut one of the last land links with the salient. In the pocket, with a perimeter of three hundred kilometers, were the bulk of the *Totenkopf*, the *290.Inf.Div.*, the *30.Inf.Div.*, the *12.Inf.Div.*, the *123.Inf.Div.* and the *32.Inf.Div.*, a total of 96,000 men. These units were subordinate to the *II.Armee-Korps* of General Walter von Brockdorff-Ahlefeldt. The *Totenkopf* troops that were in Staraya Russa, outside the pocket, were attached to *X.Armee-Korps* under General Christian Hansen.

A soldier armed with a *Mauser* rifle in a defensive position.

An SS soldier with an *MP38*.

***Totenkopf* soldiers busy carrying weapons and equipment, January 1942.**

At the end of January, *SS-Ostuf.* Meierdress's assault guns and *SS-Kampfgruppe Ullrich* were relieved from the Staraya Russa sector to be employed in the Ramuschewo area. That location was of vital importance to the Germans, being the main line of communication with the Demjansk salient. The *SS-Tot.Aufkl.-Abt.*, *SS-Kampfgruppe*

Wedenig and *1.Kp./SS-Tot.Pi.-Btl.* continued to fight in the Staraya Russa defensive belt, where they remained until March 21, 1942. In early February, *SS-Hstuf.* Markus Wedenig was mortally wounded in combat and was replaced at the head of his *Kampfgruppe* by *SS-Ostuf.* Heinrich Ohlmeier.

***Totenkopf* soldiers and a *Wehrmacht PzKpfw.III* on the Demjansk front, January 1942.**

German troops with an MG 34 on a defensive position.

SS-Kampfgruppe "Moder"

During the night of January 11, the Soviets took the village of Beglowo, southeast of Staraya Russa. By order of *X.Armee-Korps*, *Totenkopf* had to send a combat group to that sector. This *Kampfgruppe* assembled at Weretejka in frightfully cold weather. Placed under the command of *SS-Stubaf.* Paul Moder, commander of *III./SS-T.Art.-Rgt.*, it consisted of *III./SS-Tot.Inf.Rgt.3*, the *Stabs-Bttr./SS-Totenkpf.-Art.-Rgt.*, the *9.Bttr./SS-T.Art.-Rgt.* and a *Flak* detachment. The SS units attacked on January 13, moving from positions at Dupljanka and Oljschi. After being taken under Soviet artillery fire, the SS soldiers had to hug the ground in the snow for four hours without being able to move. Because of the intense cold, there were many cases of frostbite. Beglowo fell into German hands following bitter fighting. On January 15, the *Kampfgruppe* was ordered to retake the station at Neglowo, situated outside the town. The attack ended tragically: the SS troops lost 50 killed, 80 wounded and 80 evacuated with frostbite. On January 23, a Soviet attack forced the *Kampfgruppe* to abandon Neglowo and Oljschi. On the 26th, Griwka also fell. Despite the Soviet numerical superiority, the order was issued to retake that location.

SS troops fighting in the snow-covered forest (NA).

***Totenkopf* soldiers in combat, January 1942.**

A soviet mortar supporting an infantry attack.

On January 30, two assault guns under *SS-Ostuf.* Meierdress and a few motorcyclists from *SS-Kampfgruppe Kleffner* were thown into a counterattack, moving from Gortschizy. *SS-Kampfgruppe Moder* also had to take part in a counterattack against the same position, moving from Dupljanka and Weretejka. Against all expectations, the village of Griwka was retaken, with heavy losses to the Soviets as well as to the SS units. On February 3, *Kampfgruppe Moder* was again sent to reinforce the *290.Inf.Div.*, which had abandoned the village of Ljubezkoje to the enemy. The place returned to German control thanks to a counterattack made by *Totenkopf* troops.

On February 6, the Soviets captured the position at Mal. Kalinez, wrested from the *30.Inf.Div.* The *X.Armee-Korps* once again called upon *Kampfgruppe Moder*, which attacked two days later supported by only one tank from *2.Kp./Pz.Rgt.203*. The village was retaken, but the SS suffered eight killed, among whom was *SS-Stubaf.* Moder himself. On February 12, the Soviets were able again to surround the position. *Kampfgruppe* personnel, placed under command of *SS-Ostuf.* Engelbert Wisheu, were again engaged in liberating the village. That officer, who had wished to stay in service despite the loss of an arm during the French campaign, was killed while leading his men, but his unit nonetheless was able to reach the garrison. The following day, February 13, the Soviets attacked and took the towns of Dupljanka and Tschernaja. During the night, the fighting shifted to the position at Mal. Kalinez, where only fourteen survivors out of the two hundred and forty men of the garrison managed to make it back to German lines. During the day of the 14th, the fighting moved to Weretejka and Gortschizy, defended by what was left of *III./SS-Tot.Inf.Rgt.3*. All of the Soviet attacks were contained thanks to the providential appearance of the *Stukas*. On the 21st, the *290.Inf.Div.* pulled back its defensive line nerar Gortschizy. That location was lost on February 23, 1942, after furious fighting. *SS-Kampfgruppe Moder* was by that time disbanded. The forty survivors of *III./SS-Tot.Inf.Rgt.3* were integrated into *SS-Kampfgruppe Kleffner* at Wassiljewschtschina.

Totenkopf **soldiers during a withdrawal, January 1942.**

Horse-mounted scouts.

A German NCO in a defensive position.

SS-Kampfgruppe "Säumenicht"

On January 12, 1942, *X.Armee-Korps* requested *Totenkopf* to provide personnel to for immediate employment on the front line. Two days later, on January 14, a combat group was formed with two motorcycle companies placed under the command of *SS-Ostuf.* Rudolf Säumenicht. The *Kampfgruppe* was ordered to reach Jawsy, where it was to be attached to *Gruppe Leopold*, formed with army personnel. *Kampfgruppe Kleffner* was also operating in the same sector. *Gruppe Leopold* attacked the next day, moving from Redja, along the road that led to Staraya Russa. Following a promising start, the advance of the German troops was halted halfway to Staraya Russa. It was necessary to withdraw to Systschewo and establish defensive positions. The Soviets lost no time in attacking Systschewo, forcing the Germans to fall back again. Some of the *Kampfgruppe* troops who were cut off were able to reach the *Kampfgruppe Becker* lines at Woskressenskoje. Another part of the *Kampfgruppe* was wiped out during the withdrawal. The few survivors wandered for several weeks behind the Soviet lines and ended up reaching the airport at Staraya Russa, almost miraculously. The bulk of *SS-Kampfgruppe Säumenicht* was able to push on to Subakino, where it freed a *Luftwaffe* labor battalion. Soon after, it was ordered to interecept enemy movements towards the Pola River. On January 29, the Soviets captured Gonzy and used it as a jump-off point for an attack against Subakino.

A German ski unit moving into a Russian village, January 1942.

SS soldiers transporting material on special sleds.

Threatened with encirclement, the SS troops had to fall back to Dretenka. Greatly outnumbered, they had to abandon their heavy weapons in the field because of the lack of vehicles. After having passed through Gridino, on January 31 the surviving personnel of the *Kampfgruppe* reached Redzy, where gthey were ordered to hold the position at all costs. The Soviets attacked day and night and the SS troops once again found themselves cut off from their lines. Their losses were high. The *Luftwaffe* was able to air drop supplies and ammunition, although the quantities were insufficient. Medicine for the wounded was also lacking. *SS-Ostuf.* Säumenicht decided to attempt a breakout with the last hundred men fit for combat during the night of February 4, with the objective of reaching the Ramuschewo road. After an exhausting march in the deep snow and intense cold, the SS troops were within sight of the road. But, to their great disappointment, they found that the position had already been occupied by the Soviets. It was then decided to go on towards Kobylkino, where *SS-Kampfgruppe Ullrich* was located, but that *Kampfgruppe* had also been surrounded by strong Soviet forces. For *SS-Ostuf.* Säumenicht, it now seemed impossible to be able to cross through the enemy lines. He then decided to march westward, reaching the Tscherentschizy-Onufrijewo road.

***Totenkopf* troops on the march, 1942.**

A *Totenkopf* machine gun team, January 1942.

An SS machine gunner with an *MG 34*.

There they found the remains of a *Werhmacht* column that had been wiped out; most of its men had been killed with a bullet in the back of the neck. The remnants of the *Kampfgruppe* reached the German lines at Welikoje Selo, defended by *SS-Kampfgruppe Becker*. The soldiers were exhausted, many of the wounded had died along the way, especially due to the cold. After a few hours of rest, the survivors were gathered together at Leuschinka.

SS-Kampfgruppe "Becker"

On January 16, 1942, the Soviets were able to cut the Staraya Russa-Kholm road between the Robja and Porrussja rivers. After several failed attempts by *X.Armee-Korps* units, *SS-Kampfgruppe Becker* was ordered to quit its positions northwest of Staraya Russa in order to try to free the road to Kholm. The combat group under *SS-Ostubaf.* Becker consisted of the *Stab SS-T.Inf.Rgt.3*, the *Kradschützen-Bataillon*, the *IV./Luftwaffe-Feldregiment 3*, the *III./Luftwaffe-Feldregiment 5*, the *Feldersatz-Bataillon/5.leichte-Division,* the *1.Kp./Ski-Bataillon Luftflotte 1,* the *3.Kp./SS-T.Aufkl.-Abt.,* the *4.Bttr./SS-T.Art.-Rgt.* and elements of the *SS-T.Ski-Kompanie.* The *Kampfgruppe* attacked on January 26, capturing the village of Penna and continued southward, as far as Ssokolowa, which was taken on February 2. The villages that were taken during this slow advance were transformed into strongpoints, although there was no continuous contact between them because of the shortage of men.

An SS mortar squad, surrounded by ammunition cases, January 1942 (NA).

A German defensive position on the Demjansk front.

Because of that, some of them fell into Soviet hands again. Nonetheless, the *Kampfgruppe* continued its attack, turning to the east, taking the following locations: Oshedowa, Perwaja, Welikoje Selo and Onufrijewa. In Onufrijewa, *Kampfgruppe Becker* wiped out the Soviet 203rd Ski Battalion, which left a total of 441 men dead in the field at the end of the bitter battle. Soon after, however, the *Kampfgruppe* had to fall back to Ssokolowa because of strong enemy pressure. As soon as it reached its new position, it was surrounded by enemy forces that had cut the Staraya Russa road. The

Soviets attacked with infantry supported by tanks. During the fighting the German troops suffered more than two hundred wounded. Not being able to count on any outside help, Becker ordered a breakthrough move to the south through the Soviet lines. Two *PzKpfw IV* tanks of *Pz.Rgt.203* were in the lead. Every village that was crossed had to be fought over. After a harrowing march of four days through enemy lines, with no supplies and carrying more than three hundred wounded with them, on February 13, the *Kampfgruppe* managed to reach the German lines south of Dretina.

An artillery observation post on the Demjansk front, February 1942 (*Charles Trang*).

***Totenkopf* soldiers, January 1942.**

Following a few hours of rest, the remnants of the *Kampfgruppe* were again committed to combat, this time in the Kamenka sector, on both sides of Astrilowo. The Soviets attacked from the south and from the east and on February 23, were able to capture part of the area defended by *SS-Kampfgruppe Säumenicht*. *SS-Kampfgruppe Becker* then established new defensive positions between Isossimowka and Possetschischte, west of the Polist River. This defensive line was held until the end of March. On March 25, 1942, *SS-Staf.* Becker assumed command of the *Sicherungs-Regiment* (security regiment) of *X.Armee-Korps*.

Employment of "Gruppe Eicke"

In late January 1942, the Soviet 1st and 2nd Guards corps advanced southward, moving from the Redja and Lovat valleys. Their objective was to cut the Wassiljewschtschina-Bjakowo-

Omytschlino road to isolate the *II.Armee-Korps* from the *X.Armee-Korps*, which they did on 20 January. Thus, the only road left to the Germans with which to supply II.Armee-Korps was the most southerly road, which passed through Kobylkino and Salutschje. But even that road was soon threatened because *II.Armee-Korps* was being encircled from the south as well. In fact, strong Soviet forces were working their way northwest, across the swampy forests located to the east of the Lovat. The *II.Armee-Korps* and *X.Armee-Korps* could commit only improvised *Kampfgruppen* against them.

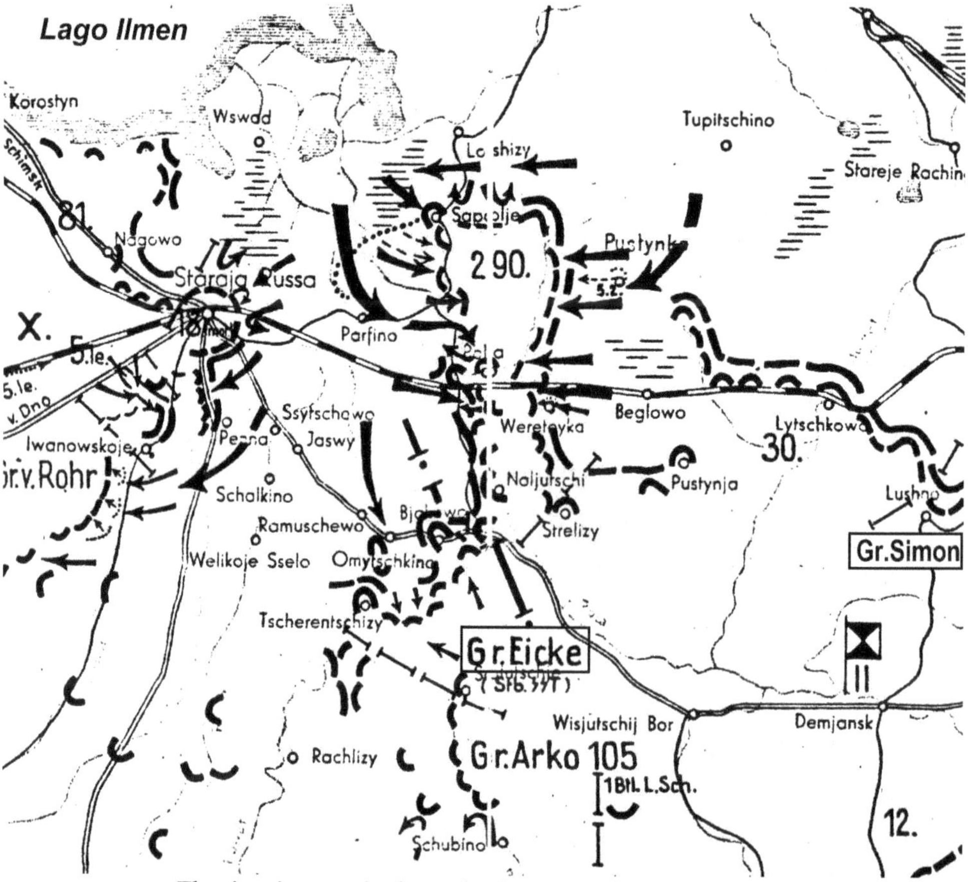

The situation map in the pocket between February 1-19, 1942.

A German defensive position with an *MG 34*.

German headquarters also ordered the formation of a new defensive front, facing west, to deal with the Soviet troops that were advancing in the rear of *II.Armee-Korps*. On February 1, Ramuschewo was taken by the Soviets and *SS-Kampfgruppe Säumenicht* was surrounded at Redzy. On February 3, General Brockdorff-Ahlefeldt decided to separate the *Totenkopf* units

January 1942: Himmler visiting *Totenkopf* troops, discussing the situation with Theodor Eicke, on the right in the photo. *SS-Ostubaf.* Lammerding is behind them.

***Totenkopf* troops during an attack.**

that were in the Demjansk pocket into two groups, *Gruppe Eicke* and *Gruppe Simon*, in order to commit them to he most threatened sectors. *Gruppe Eicke* was sent to defend a 64-kilometer front, along the line Wassiljewschtschina-Bjakowo-Kobylkino-Tscherentschizy-Salutschje, on the extreme west of the pocket. Its mission was to prevent the Soviets, who were attacking from the west, to widen the breach that separated *II.Armee-Korps* from *X.Armee-Korps*. To accomplish this mission, Eicke had the following forces at his disposal:

- Personnel of the artillery regiment and anti-tank battalion of *32.Infanterie-Division*
- A battalion of *30.Inf.Div.* (*I./Inf.Rgt.6*)
- *SS-Kampfgruppe "Wallner"* at Bol.Dubowizy
- *SS-Kampfgruppe "Kleffner"* at Wassiljewschtschina
- Remnants of *III./SS-Tot.Inf.Rgt. 3* at Gortschizy
- *SS-Kampfgruppe "Meierdress"* at Bjakowo
- *SS-Kampfgruppe "Ullrich"* at Kobylkino
- Personnel of *I./SS-Tot.Inf.Rgt.3* at Tscherentschizy

Gruppe Eicke numbered about six thousand men. It was later reinforced by several companies of the *30.Inf.Div.*, the *32.Inf.Div.*, the *12.Inf.Div.* and the *123.Inf.Div.* Having few forces at his disposal, Eicke had to settle for organizing his defense using isolated strongpoints. A peremptory order arrived from the headquarters of *II.Armee-Korps*: *"...The strongpoints must be held until the last bullet. Combat cannot be suspended nor can any position be evacuated without first receiving the order to do so. The senior officer in each strongpoint will be responsible for enforcing this order. Each house and each village that we evacuate must be burned. Only by fighting in this manner will we beat the Soviets"*.

The *Kampfgruppe* held the fate of the soldiers of *II.Armee-Korps* and *X.Armee-Korps*, and as a result, of the entire *16.Armee*, in its hands. Theodor Eicke embodied the soul of the resistance. He ordered the garrisons of the strongpoints to dig in as best they could. The SS troops had to dig trenches and individual foxholes in the frozen ground by using explosives. But even to dig in deeply was not enough to deal with a stronger enemy supported by tanks. And so, on February 6, *SS-Kampfgruppe Ullrich* was cut off at Kobylkino and the battle of Tscherentschizy cost heavy losses among the SS troops.

A *Totenkopf* defensive position in the Demjansk pocket, February 1942.

Moving supplies on sleds, February 1942.

An *MG 34* under cover in a *bunker* covered by snow.

The Soviets attempted to break through the line Bjakowo-Sakorytno-Kulakowo-Tscherentschizy, then to push to Salutschje. Nonetheless, in the days that followed the SS troops were able to block all enemy attempts to break through. On February 8, the spearheads of the Soviet 11th Army and 1st Shock Army linked up at Kobylkino and towards evening the last supply line to *II.Armee-Korps* was cut; the Demjansk salient was thus turned into a pocket. Hitler repeated the order for all of the units surrounded to hold in place while waiting for the front to stabilize to the west of the Lovat, promising a relief operation. In addition, Air Marshal Hermann Göring had given assurances that the surrounded forces could be resupplied by air. The *Reichsmarschall* kept his promise during the first two weeks: on 22 February, 110 flights carried 182 tons of food and ammunition, and the following day, a maximum of 286 tons was reached. During the weeks that followed, poor weather, action by the Soviet air force and shortage of available aircraft caused the level of resupply to fall well below the required miniumum.

Supplies being unloaded from aboard a *Junker Ju* 52.

A *Totenkopf* defensive position in the forest.

General Brockdorff-Ahlefeldt.

On February 9, fighting was heavy areound Bjakowo, Korowitschina, Kobylkino and Tscherentschizy; the last named location, which controlled the valley of the Lovat, constituted one of the toughest strongpoints of *Gruppe Eicke*. It was defended by troops of *I./SS-Tot.Inf.Rgt.3*, by *6.Kp./Inf.Rgt.46*, by *9.Kp./Inf.Rgt.6*, by a battery of the *SS-T.Art.-Rgt.*, and other personnel. On February 11, the southern front of *Gruppe Eicke* was threatened in the Salutschje sector. Eicke then requested authorization to evacuate Kobylinko in order to throw *SS-Kampfgruppe Ullrich* into a counterattack, but *II.Armee-Korps* organized the defense of Salutschje, requesting the *30.Inf.Div.*, the *32.Inf.Div.* and the *123.Inf.Div.* each to put a company at the disposition of *Gruppe Eicke*. These three companies were placed under the command of the headquarters of *II./SS-Tot.Inf.Rgt.3* and were used to form *SS-Kampfgruppe Baum*. In addition, *IV./SS-T.Art.-Rgt.* formed a combat battery (*Gefechtsbatterie*) under *SS-Ustuf.* Straatmann, with three guns from the *10., 11.* and *12.(schwere)Batterie.*

On February 15, a *Kampfgruppe* consisting of six companies under *SS-Hstuf.* Ernst Häussler, commander of *5.Kp./SS-Tot.Inf.Rgt.1*, was sent to Wersch.Sonsnowka, south fo Salutschje, to try to slow down the Soviet advance and to thus allow defensive positions to be organized at Salutschje. The Soviets attacked Kobylkino and Tscerentschizy with infantry and tanks without letup. At Kobylkino the situation continued to deteriorate. On February 22, after having put up a tenacious defense, *SS-Kampfgruppe Ullrich* abandoned the place and pulled back to Tscherentschizy. That same day, General Brockdorff-Ahlefeldt reported in the corps war diary that: "Gruppe Eicke *fought valiantly. In my eyes, the men at Kobylkino and Wassiljewschtschina and their commanders,* SS-Stubaf. *Ullrich and* SS-Stubaf. *Kleffner, are heroes*". A few hours later that same day the positions at Tscherentschizy were abandoned; the garrison withdrew to the Salutschje sector. On February 19, 1942, both Kleffner and Ullrich were officially awarded the Knight's Cross.

***SS-Stubaf.* Karl Ullrich.**

***SS-Stubaf.* Franz Kleffner.**

A *StuG.III* engaged in combat, February 1942.

The SS engineers were reinforced by a number of personnel and Karl Ullrich reorganized his *Kampfgruppe* on two battalions, commanded by *SS-Hstuf.* Dörner and Krauth. The Soviets attacked the positons of *SS-Kampfgruppe Häussler* at Werch.Sosnowka; the SS troops held their positions until February 25, when they withdrew to Salutschje. *SS-Hstuf.* Häussler was gravely wounded during the fighting and had to be evacuated. Around the end of February, the Soviets intensified their efforts to wipe out the Demjansk pocket before the

Germans could mount a relief operation. The besieged forces held up well, despite the cold, the privations and the intense bombardment by the enemy.

Soviet infantry in the attack supported by anti-tank guns.

A German NCO in winter garb.

A group of *Totenkopf* soldiers, February 1942.

The situation at Kobylkino and Korowitschino

SS-Kampfgruppe Ullrich, consisting of the bulk of the *SS-Tot.Pi.-Btl.*, the *16.(Pi.)Kp./SS-Tot.Inf.Rgt.1*, the *8.Bttr/.SS-Tot.Art.-Rgt.* and a *Flak Kampftrupp* of the *SS-Tot.Flak-Abt.*, defended the Kobylkino sector. Karl Ullrich had been ordered to hold on to this lone bridgehead on the Lowat, through which the road that led to Staraya Russa led, at all costs. It represented the only possibility for *II.Armee-Korps* to cross the river. Just to the south of Kobylkino was Korowitschino, defended by *SS-Kampfgruppe Seela*, consisting of *3.Kp./SS-T.Pi.-Btl*, the *Brücko/SS-T.Pi.-Btl.* and scattered personnel of the *12.* and *123.Infanterie-Division*. The Soviets attacked without respite and with no thought to the heavy losses they incurred. The SS were not able to reply to Soviet artillery fire because their heavy weapons lacked ammunition. On February 9, the Soviets cut off contact between Kobylkino and Tscherentschizy. Patrols were sent out to re-establish contact, but were unsuccessful. On February 11, the SS troops had to fight off a massive enemy attack supported by tanks. The German soldiers were able to fend off the Soviets who left two hundred dead on the field.

Ernst Stäudle with the rank of *Unterscharführer.*

These terrible attacks were repeated four times throughout the day. During the night between February 15-16, *SS-Stubaf.* Ullrich attempted a breakout maneuver to Tscherentschizy to enable the wounded to be evacuated; the action failed about a kilometer short of the objective. On February 20, a new attempt was crowned with success and seventy seriously wounded men were able to be transported across the Soviet lines. During the evening of February 22, the strongpoint was finally evacuated. Linkup with the garrison at Tscherentschizy was made on February 23.

The Knight's Cross for Ernst Stäudle

On February 26, after the abandonment of Kobylkino, Soviet troops continued their advance, deeply penetrating the German positions. To stop them, it was absolutely necessary to establish a new defensive front and request the support of heavy weapons. *SS-Oberscharführer* Ernst Stäudle had been detached as a forward artillery observer of the *8.Bttr./SS-T.Art.-Rgt.*; during the night between February 26-27, he was hiding in one of the houses in the small village of Schumilkino, lost in the immense snow-covered plain. The position was attacked by the Soviets following a massive bombardment by their artillery. The Soviet infantry got to within about fifty meters from Schumilkino, which was now defended by only a handful of men still able to fight. Some personnel from a construction battalion were sent to reinforce them, but as soon as they arrived, they ran off in terror as soon as they caught sight of the Soviet soldiers. Despite having been wounded in an arm and a leg, *SS-Oscha.* Stäudle placed himself at the head of the few survivors and directed fire against the packed ranks of Soviet infantry, having only a single 37 mm *Flak* gun as heavy weaponry.

Assault guns moving towards the Jawsy area.

SS-Hstuf. **Max Seela.**

The fire from the *Flak* gun allowed the Soviet attack to be repulsed and to ease the threat against the rear area of the Salutschje garrison. *SS-Oscha.* Stäudle, lacking strength and gravely wounded, was finally evacuated to the rear. Already decorated with both classes of the Iron Cross, on 10 April 1942 he was awarded the Knight's Cross. Weakened by the serious wounds he had sustained in combat, he was not able to return to his unit and following a lengthy hospital convalescence he was assigned to the SS artillery school at Beneschau, in the Protectorate of Bohemia and Moravia.

The Knight's Cross for Max Seela

On March 1, 1942, the commander of the *Totenkopf* recommended Max Seela for the Knight's Cross for his heroism and valor demonstrated in battle. The award was officially granted to him on 3 May 1942. Following is the citation written by the commander of the *Totenkopf, SS-Gruf.* Theodor Eicke: *"…Upon his return to Staraya Russa at the beginning of January, following a period of convalescence,* SS-Hauptsturmführer *Seela quickly entered into action and with a company defended the village of Lipowitzy, situated southeast of Staraya Russa. After the Soviets had broken through the front along the Lovat at the end of January, SS-Hstuf. Seela fought as part of* Gruppe Ullrich *and defended Korowitschina until 24 February 1942. Although the Soviets had attacked with many tanks supported by violent artillery fire and aircraft, with the aim of capturing the southern sector of the location,* SS-Hstuf. *Seela prevented the breakthrough of the enemy troops into the area and captured the bridge over the Lovat after heroic fighting. Despite the heavy losses and the lack of adequate reinforcementsby air drop to the group that was by then surrounded,* SS-Hstuf. *Seela continued to push his exhausted men to hold on and to respond with counterattacks against the Soviet assaults from three different directions. When on 24 February 1942 the order was given for the surrounded combat group to withdraw,* SS-Hstuf. *Seela, although wounded, led the withdrawal of the rear guard and brought it to new positions. I ask that* SS-Hauptsturmführer *Seela be awarded the Knight's Cross of the Iron Cross in recognition of his heroic behavior and his success in the fighting cited above".*

Bibliography

M. Afiero, "*Totenkopf*", Marvia Edizioni

M. Afiero, "*3.SS-Pz.Div. Totenkopf - Vol. I: 1939-1943*", Associazione Culturale Ritterkreuz

M. Afiero, "*The 3rd Waffen-SS Pz.Div. Totenkopf 1939-1943: Vol.1*", Schiffer Publishing

M. Afiero, "*Totenkopf I: 1939-1942*", Almena Ediciones

Recruiting centres/offices of the Italian SS in Italy

By Hugh Page Taylor

Colour postcards of Gino Boccasile's(1) "submachine gun and dagger", "3 fingers" and "the bugler" illustrations for the Italian SS. Of these, the "submachine gun and dagger" is stamped with the message "Gift of the Italian SS Legion". Full colour versions as well as simple monochrome sketches based on these designs were used extensively in posters, postcards and flyers distributed by the recruiting centres/offices.

Recruiting offices of the Italian SS in Italy

Under a central Recruiting Centre (*Centro di Reclutamento*) in Cremona, 29 subordinate centres were established in capital towns of the majority of provinces making up the ten regions of the RSI by an order dated 18 February 1944. Whereas the central Centre was unnumbered, the others were identified by Roman numerals as follows:

Number	Town	Region
-	Cremona	Lombardia (Lombardy)
I	Savona	Liguria
II	Cuneo	Piemonte (Piedmont)
III	Torino (Turin)	-"-
IV	Alessandria	-"-
V	Aosta	Valle d'Aosta (Aosta Valley)
VI	Novara	Piemonte (Piedmont)
VII	Como	Lombardia (Lombardy)
VIII	Milano (Milan)	-"-
IX	Bergamo	-"-
X	Brescia	-"-
XI	Verona	Veneto
XII	Mantova (Mantua)	Lombardia (Lombardy)
XIII	Treviso	Veneto
XIV	Padova (Padua)	-"-
XV	Bologna	Emilia-Romagna
XVI	Modena	-"-
XVII	Firenze (Florence)	Toscana (Tuscany)
XVIII	Forlì	Emilia-Romagna
XIX	Ancona	Marche (The Marshes)
XX	Macerata	-"-
XXI	Perugia	Umbria
XXII	Viterbo	Lazio
XXIII	Grosseto	Toscana (Tuscany)
XXIV	Siena	-"-
XXV	Pisa	-"-
XXVI	Apuania (Massa-Carrara)	-"-
XXVII	Genova (Genoa)	Liguria
XXVIII	Parma	Emilia-Romagna
XXIX[2]	Bolzano	Alto Adige (South Tyrol)

The regions of the RSI and two Operation Zones.

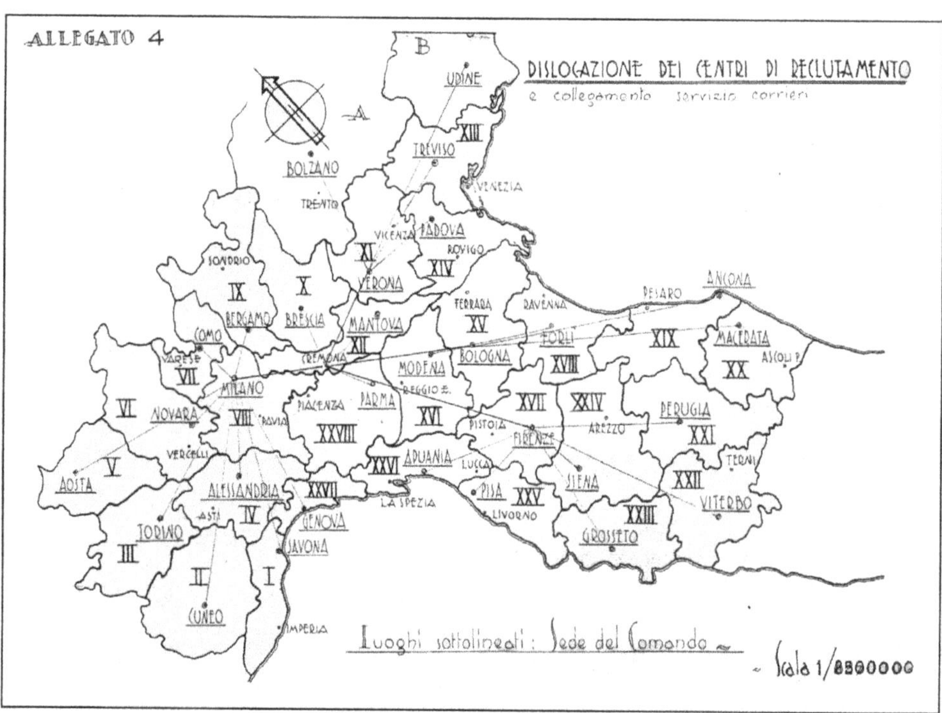

Map of the Recruitment Centres, undated, but believed to have been drawn up by the Personnel Office of what was at that time known generically as the Italian SS Legion (Legione SS Italiana) as Attachment 4 to an otherwise unidentified document in the spring of 1944. Towns where Commands were located are underlined and the connecting lines radiating out of Cremona, Milan and Florence show links served by a courier service, not necessarily hierarchical subordination. This map was first published on page 68 of what is unquestionably the best book written to date on the Italian SS: *"Sentire – Pensare – Volere"* by Corbatti and Nava.

There are notable omissions from the map:

- Bolzano: The Recruitment Centre in this the capital of South Tyrol (Alto Adige to the Italians), 96 miles (154 km) north of Verona, was underlined to show the presence of an as yet unnumbered Command (*Comando*). According to one historian, however, "Bozen (*Alpenvorland*)" was listed as the XXIXth on the list authorised by the Germans(3). The initial absence of a number may have been due to the fact that the Bolzano province was a part of one of the two so-called "Operational Zones" (*Zone di Operazioni* in Italian, and *Operationszonen* in German) in northeastern Italy that were not technically parts of the Italian Social Republic (*Repubblica Sociale Italiana*, or RSI). These had been ordered by Hitler on 10 September 1943 and were called the "Pre-Alps" (*Zona delle Prealpi*, or *Alpenvorland* – abbrviated as OZAV), comprising the provinces of Belluno, Bolzano and Trento, and the "Adriatic Litoral" (*Litorale Adriatico*, or *Adriatisches Küstenland* – OZAK), with the provinces of Fiume, Gorizia, Pola, Trieste and Udine. The two Zones were subject to total German military control, and between them created what was considered a reliable defensive barrier between the German (former Austrian) southern border and northeastern Italy. In theory the two Zones remained under Italian sovereignty and were only to remain under German military control for the duration of the war, but in fact it is likely that Hitler had annexation in mind.

- Busto Arsizio: There was an enrolment centre (*Centro Arruolamento*) in this town in the Province of Varese, some 22 miles (35 km) north of Milan

- Pavia: There was what was being called an enrolment centre and then an enrolment office on 30 September and 7 October 1944 respectively in this, the capital town of the Province, some 26 miles (46 km) by road south of Milan.

- Pistoia: There was an enrolment centre at the Federation of Republican Fasces in this, the capital town of the Province, some 26 miles (42 km) northwest of Florence

- Rome (Roma): Although Viterbo in the Lazio Region was included and numbered XXII, for some reason Rome – some 50 miles (80 km) to the southsoutheast – was not shown, even though it is known to have had a secondary enrolment centre prior to the capital's liberation on 4 June 1944.

- Udine: This provincial capital is 82 miles (132 km) by road northeast of Venice and was also not numbered as it was one of the provinces making up the OZAK - see above under Bolzano.

- Varese: First an enrolment centre and then an enrolment office were listed on 30 September and 7 October 1944 respectively in this, the capital town of the Province, 36 miles (58 km) northwest of Milan. At one time it was also known as the Varese Enrolment Section of the Armed Italian SS Units (*Sezione Arruolamento Varese Unitá Armate Italiane SS*).

- Venice (Venezia): First an enrolment centre and then an enrolment office were listed on 30 September and 7 October 1944 respectively in this, the capital town of the Province, 168 miles (270 km) east of Milan.

- Vercelli: In March 1944 the Novara enrolment centre was also responsible for recruitment in the Province of Vercelli, the capital town of which was 15 miles (25 km) to the southwest of Novara.

It is also worthy of note that:

- Aosta and Cuneo: at some time recruiting from these provinces came under Turin
- Cuneo: – see under Aosta and Cuneo
- Milan: had 3 enrolment centres/offices
- Turin: – see under Aosta and Cuneo.

More information is provided in an in-depth study of the Italian SS by the English historian Edward Youngs in what would be a most welcome and ground-breaking book were it to be published (see Bibliography). Youngs provides another list with the following introduction:

"On 11 March 1944 the *Inspektion-Freiwilligen-Werbung* (Inspectorate of Recruitment), under the control of *Generalmajor* Piero Mannelli, opened 29 principal/primary *Werbstelle* (Recruitment Centres), in order to promote the enlistment of new volunteers into the ranks of the *SS Italiane*(4). Principal recruitment centres were established in Milan, Verona, Bologna and Florence, with an additional main centre at Cremona, attached to the *Rekruten-Auffang-Depot*. Each of these was served by a network of primary and secondary centres, which were based in cities and towns across Central and Northern Italy. These *Werbestelle* are listed as follows".

His list being as follows:

Principal Centres	Primary Centres Region	Primary Centres City / Town	Secondary Centres City / Town
Milan (Lombardia)	Piemonte:-	Alessandria	
		Aosta	
		Cuneo	
		Turin	
		Novara	
	Lombardia:-	Como	Varese
		Bergamo	Pavia
	Liguria:-	Genoa	
		Savona	
Cremona (main) (Lombardia) *Rekruten-Auffang-Depot*	Lombardia:-	Brescia	
		Mantova	
	Emilia Romagna:-	Parma	
Verona (Veneto)	Veneto:-	Padova	Venice
		Treviso	
	Voralpenland:-	Bozen	

	(Alpenvorland) (Bolzano) Trentino – Alto Adige	
Bologna (Emilia Romagna)	Emilia Romagna:- Modena Forlì	
	Marche:- Ancona Macerata	Pesaro
Florence (Toscana)	Toscana:-Apuania Massa (Massa-Carrara) Grosseto Pisa Siena	
	Umbria:-Perugia	
	Lazio:- Viterbo	Rome

LA

LEGIONE SS ITALIANA

chiama a raccolta i migliori

Occorrono

onore, coraggio, fedeltà

Le Brigate d'assalto

"VENDETTA" "PATRIA" "ITALIA"

saranno inquadrate coi più moderni e potenti armamenti e i migliori istruttori. Trattamento delle Forze armate germaniche. **ARRUOLATEVI**

Attuali Centri di arruolamento

ALESSANDRIA - Via Modena, 5
ANCONA - presso la Ortskommandantur
AOSTA - Palazzo Littorio
APUANIA MASSA - Viale Litoraneo, 38
BERGAMO - Via G. Negri, 2
BOLOGNA - Via Saragozza, 81 - Centro Mobilitazione
BRESCIA - Via Spalto San Marco, 3
COMO - Via Borgovico, 11
CREMONA - Palazzo della Rivoluzione
CUNEO - Caserma Vitt. Eman. II
FIRENZE - Via Fiume, 14 - 1° piano
FORLI' - C.so Diaz, 17 - 1° piano
GENOVA - Via Assarotti, 20 - int. 6
GROSSETO - Via Lanza - Villa Pallini
MACERATA - presso Casa del Fascio
MANTOVA - Via Giov. Arrivabene, 2
MILANO - Via Maestri, 2 (Viale Bianca Maria)
MODENA - Via Gaetano Tovoni, 40
NOVARA - Via Liceo Carlo Alberto, 2
PADOVA - Via Galileo Galilei, 2
PARMA - Viale Marconi, 4
PERUGIA - Albergo Brufani, cam. 52
PISA - Via XXIV Maggio, 41
SAVONA - Federaz. Repubblicana
SIENA - P.zza Unità Italiana (OND)
TREVISO - Via S. Margherita, 27
VERONA - Via P.te Raffiolo, 4, 2° p.
VITERBO - pr. Feder. Repubblicana

List of recruiting centers published in the Italian SS newspaper "*Avanguardia*" on 8 April 1944. 28 are listed, with Turin absent for some inexplicable reason.

This list includes 4 towns not given in the list of numbered centres (Pavia, Rome, Varese, and Venice), but not a further 4 that have been identified and are detailed below (Busto Arsizio, Pistoia, Udine, and Vercelli). Cremona was the supreme authority insofar as recruitment for the Italian SS was concerned, as it was there in February 1944 that the Swiss *SS-Standartenführer* Johann Eugen Corrodi von Elfenau established the recruitment depot (Deposito Reclute) for the entire Italian SS with his 61st Order of the Day (*Tagesbefehl Nr. 61*). To sum up, the depot was served by 5 principal recruiting centres, one of which also in Cremona itself (although also referred to as a secondary centre), and the others in Bologna, Florence, Milan and Verona. Primary Centres came under the principal centres: under Bologna came Ancona, Forlì, Macerata, and Modena; under Cremona: Brescia, Mantua and Parma; under Florence: Apuania (today Massa Carrara), Grosseto, Perugia, Pisa, Siena and Viterbo; under Milan: Alessandria, Aosta, Bergamo, Como,

Cuneo, Genoa, Savona and Turin, and under Verona: Bolzano, Padua, Treviso, and possibly Udine (also the recruituing center for the *24. Waffen-Gebirgs-(Karstjäger) Division der SS*). Secondary Centres were under Bologna (Pesaro), Florence (Rome) and Milan (Pavia and Varese).

List of the 13 remaining recruiting centres published in "*Avanguardia*" on 30 September 1944, illustrated by Boccasile's "submachine gun and dagger".

The names of the centres changed to match those given to what was generically referred to as "the Italian SS" (*le SS italiane*) or the "Italian SS Legion" (*La Legione SS Italiana*) and the following have been confirmed from contemporary documents, although others were possibly used: "Armed Militia" (*Waffen-Miliz - Milizia Armata,* indicating the link with the Waffen-SS), "Italian Volunteer Legions" (*Legioni Volontari Italiani – Ital. Freiw. Legionen* - from between at least 20 March and 25 April 1944), "Armed Italian Units of the SS" (*Unità Armate Italiane delle SS - Italienische Waffenverbände der SS* - confirmed as at 10 June 1944), *1. Italienische Freiw.-Sturm-Brigade Milizia Armata (Pol.), 1. Sturmbrigade Italienische Freiwilligen-Legion, Waffen-Grenadier-Brigade SS (italienische Nr. 1)* and finally (although under strength and so only a division on paper) *29. Waffen-Grenadier-Division der SS (italienische Nr. 1)*. The Centres were spread around that part of central and northern Italy that remained under German control and which formed the RSI. As seen above, exceptions to this were the two Operational Zones in the northeast of the country, the "Pre-Alps" (OZAV) and the "Adriatic Litoral" (OZAK), which pending proposed annexation to Germany after an Axis victory, were under German command. Only one Recruiting Center for the Italian SS is confirmed to have existed in these areas, in the capital of the OZAV, Bolzano, and there was none in the OZAK capital of Triest.

The same 13 recruiting centres appear on this list, which appeared in "Avanguardia" on 7 October 1944, but illustrated by Boccasile's "3 fingers" design.

Whereas the German term *Werbestelle* appears to have been used throughout, the Italian terminology varied during the life of the Italian SS. Lists suggest that at first the name Recruitment Centre (*Centro di Reclutamento*) was used, which was then changed in March 1944 to Enrolment Centre (*Centro d'Arruolamento*) and finally – possibly in late September/early October 1944 – to Enrolment Office (*Ufficio d'Arruolamento*). Whether rules as to terminology were strictly dictated and/or respected is not known and one Enrolment Service (*Servizio Arruolamento Varese – Unità Armate Italiane SS*) has been identified in Varese, as well as one Sub-Section (*Sottosezione*) in Padua.

As the Allied armies advanced up the boot of Italy, centers/offices closed and their personnel were transferred further to the north. Although a Centre was formed in Rome in early March 1944, this had to shut down before the US Army liberated the capital just three months later on 4 June and the rule was to have no others south of a line drawn between Viterbo on the Mediterranean and Ascoli Piceno on the Adriatic Sea sides of Italy respectively. The gradual shrinking of the RSI was reflected in the lists of centers: a total of 28 being shown at the beginning of April 1944, but which reduced to 13 in lists published at the end of September, early October and on 23 December 1944.

A rare poster incorporating two of Boccasile's works, drawings and photographs.

For ease of reference, the offices/centres are listed in alphabetical order, by region and then province. For the sake of convenience and to contain length, only the English titles recruiting centre (*centro di reclutamento*), enrolment centre (*centro ad'arruolamento*) and enrolment office (*ufficio d'arruolamento*) will be used below.

EMILIA ROMAGNA (EMILIEN)

BOLOGNA

Formed on 25 March 1944 as Recruiting Centre XV in the Mobilization Centre (*Centro mobilitazione*) at Via Saragozza 81, but subsequently transferred to the headquarters of the Republican Fascist Federation (*Federazione Repubblicana*) at Via Manzoni 4. The Bologna Centre came hierarchically under Verona and in its turn was responsible for the centres in Ancona, Forlì, Macerata, Modena and Pesaro. It was listed as an Enrolment Centre on 8 April 1944, but was not included in lists published on 30 September and 7 October 1944. Bologna was liberated on 20/21 April 1945.

Officer in charge: *Tenente* Ermes Bacchilega.

CASTELFRANCO EMILIA

This town is some 16 miles (25 km) NW of Bologna and in September 1944 is reported to have been the location of a "Special SS Legion Command" (*Comando Legione Speciale SS*), composed of volunteer battalions named "Gorga". Other than this call for Italian volunteers, no details are available and why the name Gorga (a town in the Province of Lazio, some 37 miles [60 km] SW of Rome) should have been chosen is not known and whether there was in fact a recruiting office or centre in Castelfranco Emilia.

ITALIANI!

Il nemico, localizzato nelle posizioni raggiunte a prezzo di sanguinose perdite, benchè abbia scagliato nell'immane lotta tutta la sua potenza bellica, è costretto alla quasi immobilità, di fronte alla superiorità eroica dei soldati di Kesselring.

Il nemico sa che lo arrestarsi gli sarà fatale.

Il nemico sa che i nostri battaglioni, i battaglioni che risulteranno le ferree unità destinate a stupire il mondo tutto, stanno per essere lanciate a tutto travolgere.

Soldati di mille Battaglie e di mille Eroismi, *inquadratevi!*

Italiani di tutte le classi e di tutti i ceti, *avanti!*

Laddove è da impugnare un'arma, è la dignità e l'onore.

Là è il ritorno alla vita!

Là è la gloria!

ITALIANI!

L'ora dell'ultimo combattimento sta per scoccare.

Quell'ora — deve — sarà — la nostra ora!

Recruiting leaflet published in September 1944 (the XXIInd year of the Fascist Era) by the Headquarters of a Special SS Legion, consisting of Volunteer Battalions named "*Gorga*". No such Legion or Battalions are listed in books or magazine articles written about the Italian SS, such as the works of Corbatti/Nava, Lazzero and Youngs.

FORLÌ

Formed as Recruiting Centre XVIII at Via Garibaldi 15, but subsequently transferred to the first floor of Corso Diaz 17. Hierarchically under Bologna, it was listed as an Enrolment Centre on 8 April 1944, but was not included in lists dated 30 September and 7 October 1944. Forlì was liberated on 10 November 1944.

Officer in charge: *Capitano/Waffen-Hauptsturmführer* Bruno Zanella.

MODENA

Formed as Recruiting Centre XVI at the "Garibaldi" army barracks and subsequently transferred to Via Gaetano Tavoni 40. Hierarchically under Bologna, it was listed as an Enrolment Centre on 8 April 1944, but was not included in lists dated 30 September and 7 October 1944. Modena was liberated on 21/22 April 1945.

Officer in charge: *Capitano* Giacomo Sacchi.

PARMA

Listed as an unnumbered enrolment centre for the Italian SS Legion (*Centro arruolamento Legione SS Italiana*) already by 6 January 1944, it was subsequently numbered as Recruitment Centre XXVII and located at Viale Marconi 4. Hierarchically subordinate to Cremona, it was listed as an enrolment centre on 8 April 1944, but was not included in lists dated 30 September and 7 October 1944. Parma was liberated on 24/25 April 1945.

Officer in charge: *Maggiore* Silvio Finadri.

Legione SS Italiana

Per l'onore e l'indipendenza della Patria, per il vostro benessere, per la vostra libertà di cittadini italiani, seguite l'esempio delle Divisioni volontarie che si preparano alla riscossa.

Date prova di coraggio e di coscienza patriottica.

Arruolatevi nella Legione S.S. Italiana.

Il trattamento economico è uguale a quello delle S.S. germaniche. L'addestramento avviene in Italia. Il Centro arruolamento è a Parma (viale Marconi n. 4).

Cutting from the Parma newspaper "Gazzetta di Parma" of 6 January 1944.

LATIUM (LAZIO)

ROME (ROMA, ROM)

The poster in the center of this group on a wall in Rome is for the Italian SS Legion. It refers to fighting at the Nettuno bridgehead and so must date from February to late May 1944, as Rome was liberated by the US Army on 4 June that year.

Given Rome's importance in February/March 1944, it is curious that only a secondary office should have been formed there at the headquarters of the Republican Fascist Federation on the 4th floor of Via Veneto 31, a decision possibly taken in anticipation of the Allied break-out from the bridgehead at Anzio-Nettuno, following the landing there by the US Army on 22 January. Government ministries had in fact already been evacuated to the north and Rome was liberated between 4 and 6 June 1944.

Officer in charge: Not identified.

VITERBO

Formed as Recruiting Centre XXII at the headquarters of the Republican Fascist Federation. Despite being in the Province of Lazio, it was hierarchically subordinate to the Tuscan capital of Florence and was listed as an enrolment centre on 8 April 1944. Viterbo was liberated on 9/10 June 1944.

Officer in charge: *Capitano* Orlando Giordano.

LIGURIA (LIGURIEN)

GENOA (GENOVA, GENUA)

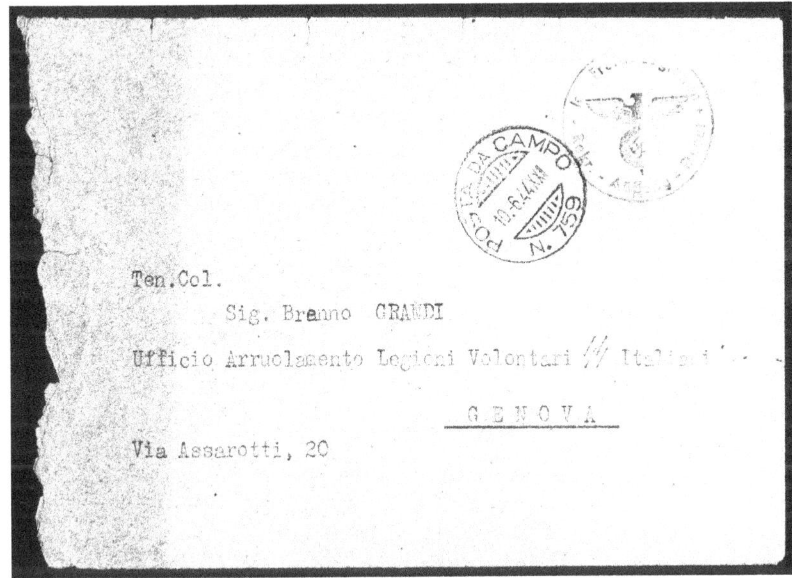

Envelope posted on 10 June 1944 to Tenente Colonello Brenno Grandi of the Recruitment Office of the Italian SS Legions in Genoa by Tenente Colonello Tiberio Bedotti of the central Depot in Cremona.

Formed as Recruiting Centre XVII at Via Assarotti 20, internal 6, it was hierarchically subordinate to Milan. Listed as an enrolment centre on 8 April 1944, this had been changed to enrolment office by 10 June 1944. Although not liberated until April 1945, it did not appear in lists dated 30 September and 7 October 1944. Genoa was liberated on 23/26 April 1945. Officer in charge: *Capitano/Waffen-Hauptsturmführer* Francesco Gnata.

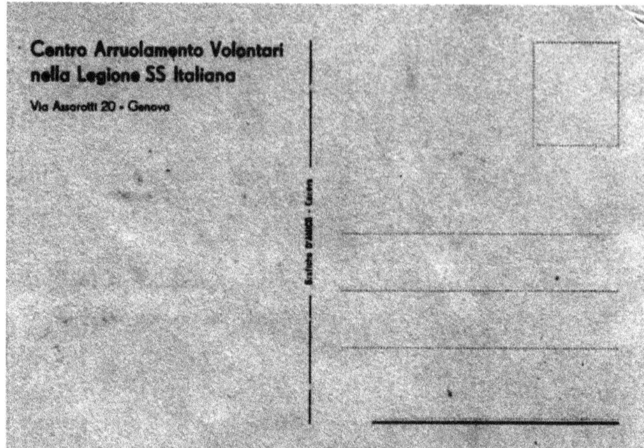

Field postcard with Boccasile's "bugler" design and indication of the Volunteers Enrolment Centre in Via Assarotti 20 in Genoa.

SAVONA

Formed as Recruiting Centre I at the headquarters of the Republican Fascist Federation in Piazza Mentana, it was hierarchically subordinate to Milan. Listed as an enrolment centre 8 April 1944, it was not included in lists dated 30 September and 7 October 1944. Savona was liberated on 25 April 1945.

Officer in charge: *Tenente* Ottorino Montanari.

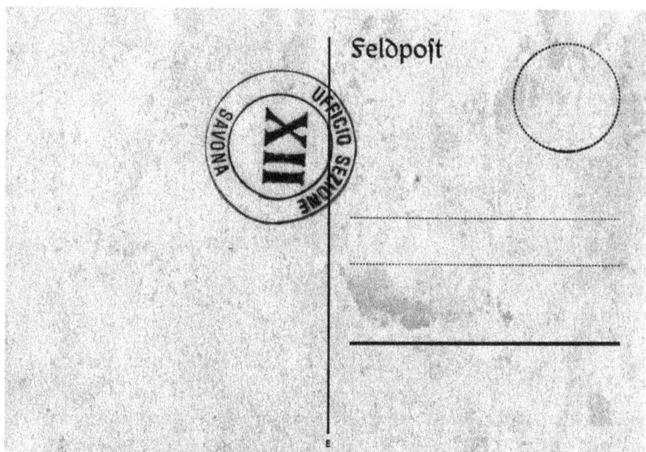

This field postcard was issued by the German Propaganda Department (Propaganda-Staffel) under reference IV/127. Although making no reference to the Italian SS Legion, the heroic volunteer wears an SS collar patch. The significance of the circular ink stamp "Ufficio Sezione XII Savona" on the reverse is not known, and does not correspond to the number given to the recruiting office in Savona, which was "I".

LOMBARDY (LOMBARDIA)

BERGAMO

Formed as Recruiting Centre IX for the Italian Volunteer SS Legion (*Legione Volontari S.S. italiani/Legione SS Italiana*) at the Casa Littoria, Via G. Negri 2, but subsequently transferred to Via XX Settembre 1 where it was shown as the enrolment office for the *Legione SS Italiana*. Hierarchically under Milan, it was listed as an enrolment centre on 8 April 1944, but was not included in lists dated 30 September and 7 October 1944. Its duties may have been transferred 75 miles (120 km) by road due north to Sondrio before the war ended. Bergamo was liberated on 29 April 1945.

Officer in charge: *Tenente* Agostino[5] Luzzi.

Boccasile's "3 fingers" design illustrates this leaflet, which bears an ink stamp for the enrolment center of the Italian SS Legion in Bergamo.

BRESCIA

Formed as Recruiting Centre X in Via Spalto S. Marco 3, but subsequently transferred to the headquarters of the "Benito Mussolini" Fascist District Group (*Gruppo Rionale Fascista*, or GRF) on the 2nd floor of Corso Zanardelli 30[6]. Hierarchically subordinate to Cremona, it was listed as an enrolment centre on 8 April and 30 September 1944, and rather curiously in the plural as enrolment offices (*Uffici d'arruolamento*) on 7 October 1944. It was confirmed as still active on 23 December 1944. Brescia was liberated on 25 April 1945.

Officer in charge: *Tenente* Floriano Taglieri.

Boccasile's "submachine gun and dagger" design illustrates this leaflet for the recruiting office in Brescia, which curiously shows "offices" in the plural (Corbatti/Nava).

BUSTO ARSIZIO

This is a town and municipality in the Province of Varese, where there was an SS Enrolment Centre (*Centro Arruolamento SS*) at Vicolo Custodi 2, on the corner with Via Montebello. Busto Arsizio was liberated on 25 April 1945.

Officer in charge: Unidentified

COMO

Formed as Recruiting Centre VII at the headquarters of the Republican Fascist Federation in Via Borgovico 1, it was hierarchically subordinate to Milan and listed as an enrolment centre 8 April 1944 and 30 September 1944, although subsequently listed as an enrolment office on 7 October 1944. During its existance it was transferred first to army barracks at Via Anzani 9 and finally to Piazza Cavour 9, where it was confirmed as an enrolment office on 23 December 1944. Como was liberated in late April 1945, after Mussolini had passed through the town on the 25/26 April in his futile attempt to escape to Switzerland.

Officer in charge: *Tenente* Rodolfo Macchitelli.

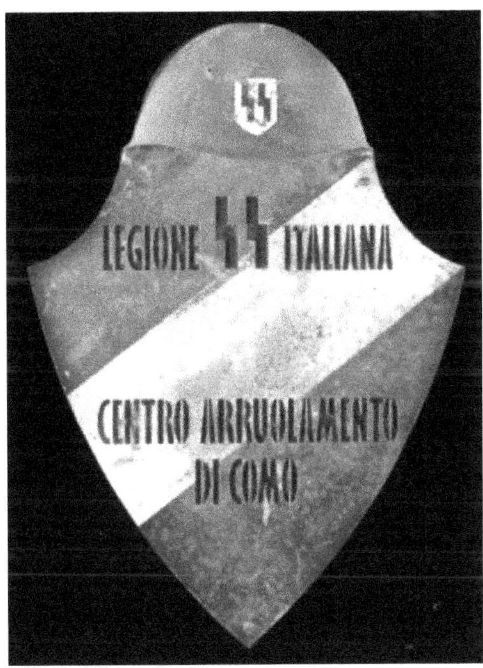

Sign for the enrolment centre in Como. It measures 69 cm x 49.5 cm.

CREMONA

Cremona was the central hub of recruitment for Italians in the *Waffen-SS*. It was the location of the Recruitment and Medical Commission of the Italian Volunteer Legions (*Commissione Reclutamento e Sanitaria delle Legioni volontari italiani*) under *Waffen-Brigadeführer und Generalmajor der Waffen-SS* Piero Mannelli as Inspector from February 1944 and the SS Recruits Reception Depot of the Italian Formations (*SS-Rekruten-Auffang-Depot der italienischen Verbande – Deposito Raggruppamento Reclute delle Legioni volontari italiani*), formed on 18 February 1944, first under *Tenente Colonnello* Tiberio Bedotti (confirmed as such at 28 February 1944) and then *Tenente Colonnello* Oreste Gardini. This depot was located at the "Col di Lana" army barracks and consisted of an HQ Company (*Compagnia Comando*), a Recruits Battalion (*Battaglione Reclute*), a Convalescents Company (*Compagnia Convalescenti*) and Central Store (*Magazzino Centrale*). The depot had Italian field post number 759 and received recruits from all of the other recruiting centres and gave them two months' basic training, following which they took the oath to Hitler as *Führer* and were assigned to the various battalions and other elements of the Italian SS. The Recuiting Centre in Cremona was unnumbered and listed as an enrolment centre on 8 April and 30 September 1944, but its name had been changed to an enrolment office in a list of 7 October 1944.

Officer in charge of the Recruiting Office (*Capo Ufficio Arruolamento*): *Maggiore* Vito VOLPE.

A secondary enrolment centre (*centro d'arruolamento secondaria*) was formed in the second half of February 1944 and opened in early March at the Palazzo della Rivoluzione in Via

Ettore Muti 20. Although reported to have been moved to Piazza Littorio 8, it was still listed as being at the original address on 23 December 1944.

Officer in charge: Not identified.

In late April 1944 all of the elements in Cremona came under a new command that was formed to provide better training, although this change was not made official until 7 September 1944. This was the Reserve Units Command of the Italian Armed Units of the SS (*Comando Unità di Riserva delle Unità Armate Italiane delle SS – Kommandostab Ersatz Einheiten der italienischen Waffenverbände der SS*) under *SS-Sturmbannführer* Luis Thaler. Cremona was liberated on 25 April 1945, but Thaler and his men had been forced to relocate to Rodengo-Saiano near Brescia on 13 January 1945 as a result of heavy Allied bombing.

Italian horizontal and German circular ink stamps on the back of an envelope sent on 10 June 1944 by Tenente Colonello Tiberio Bedotti from the H.Q. of the Recruits Reception Depot of the Italian SS Legions (Comando Raggruppamento Reclute Legioni Volontari SS Italiani – ***Rekr.-Auffang-Depot, Ital. Freiw.Legionen*****) in Cremona (Italian field post office 759).**

MANTUA (MANTOVA)

Formed as Recruiting Centre XII in Via Giovanni Arrivabene 2, it was hierarchically subordinate to Cremona and listed as an enrolment centre on 8 April and 30 September, but the name was shown as an enrolment office on 7 October and 23 December 1944. Mantua was liberated in April 1945.

Officer in charge: *Tenente Colonello* Giuseppe Soresina.

MILAN (MILANO, MAILAND)

Although Milan was not the seat of government, it was certainly the *de facto* strategic capital of the RSI. 8 recruiting centres/enrolment offices were hierarchically subordinate to it (Alessandria, Aosta, Bergamo, Como, Cuneo, Genoa, Savona, and Turin) and the high volume of volunteers who came from and around the Lombardy capital explains why it was unique in having more than one recruiting centre/enlistment centre/office for the Italian SS. The first was a recruiting office raised for men of between 17 and 35 years of age for the 1st Italian SS Regiment (*Ufficio Reclutamento del 1° Reggimento S.S. Italiana*) at the Bicocca barracks in Milan's Viale Suzzani, 125. *Colonnello* Paolo De Maria was the regimental commander, but the identity of the officer in charge of the office is not known.

COMANDO 1° REGGIMENTO

S. S. ITALIANA

MILANO

Sono aperti gli arruolamenti per la **S. S. ITALIANA** per tutti i giovani dai 17 ai 35 anni.

Giovani Italiani che avete il culto della Patria e che nel vostro cuore covate l'odio contro gli Anglo-Americani, accorrete in massa a questo nuovo CORPO ARMATO che è, e sarà sempre, l'espressione purissima militare e guerriera dell'Italia Repubblicana.

La S. S. ITALIANA per ora ha una sola ambizione: quella di affiancarsi nel più breve tempo possibile ai Camerati Germanici nel duro ma doveroso compito di liberare quella parte del nostro Patrio suolo che soffre sotto il giogo dei plutocrati.

Studenti, abbandonate le aule ed accorrete ad arruolarvi in questo nuovo Corpo Armato Ardito destinato a scrivere nella Storia le più belle pagine di eroismo per la santa lotta che ridarà alla nostra ITALIA il suo antico volto Imperiale.

Lavoratori delle officine e dei campi, arruolatevi. Solo così salverete la PATRIA ed il vostro lavoro che altrimenti sarà boicottato e svalorizzato dalle industrie Anglo-Americane.

Giovani tutti, accorrete ricordandovi che salvare la PATRIA significa salvare la Religione, la famiglia ed il lavoro: voi sapete in quanta e quale considerazione sia tenuto dai nemici questo trinomio: essi ci combattono perchè noi difendiamo queste tre sublimi verità della vita.

Nessun indugio, nessun legame familiare, nessun interesse egoistico, nessun dovere deve trattenervi, poichè quelle cose che vi sono care oggi e dalle quali non sapete o non potete staccarvi non varranno più nulla se domani non si inquadreranno nella realtà di una PATRIA libera, indipendente e sopratutto onorata.

Nella Caserma BICOCCA, in Milano (Viale Suzzani, 125) vi è l'Ufficio Reclutamento del I° Reggimento S. S. Italiana, dove potete presentarvi per l'immediato arruolamento.

EVVIVA IL DUCE

Colonnello **De Maria Paolo**

1944 recruiting leaflet or poster issued by the Headquarters of the 1st Italian SS Regiment, inviting volunteers to attend at the Bicocca Barracks in Milan's Viale Suzzani 125.

The precise date this flyer was printed is not known, but must have been before De Maria gave up his command of the 1st Regiment on 24 February 1944 to take on the role of Inspector of the Italian SS Legions.

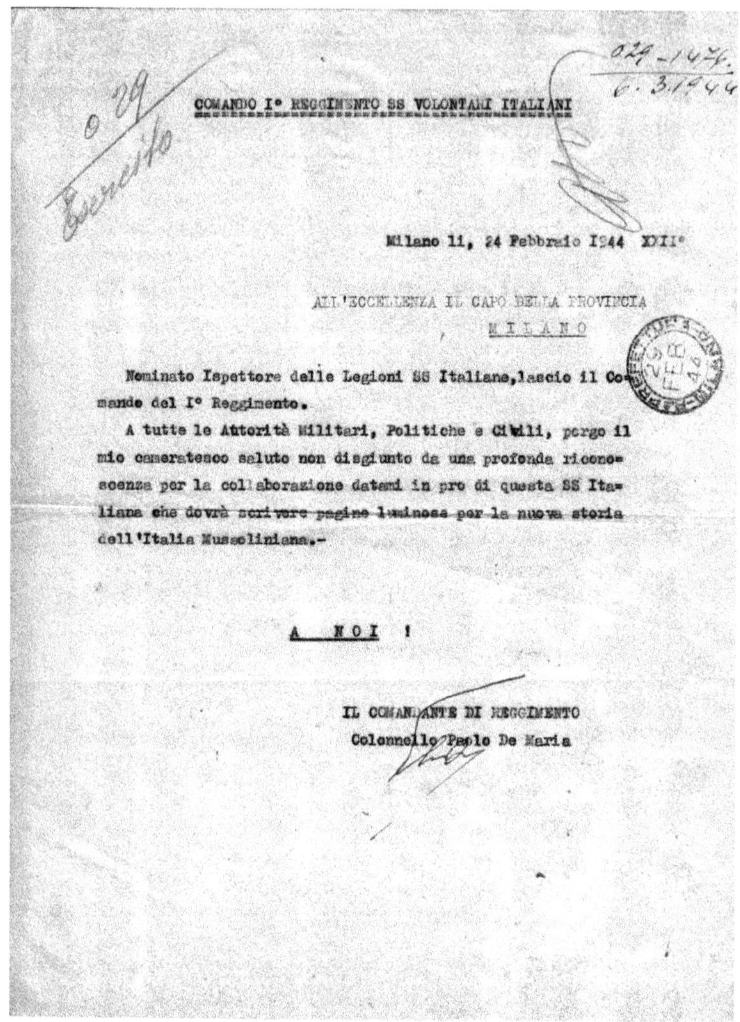

COMANDO I° REGGIMENTO SS VOLONTARI ITALIANI

Milano li, 24 Febbraio 1944 XXII°

ALL'ECCELLENZA IL CAPO DELLA PROVINCIA
MILANO

Nominato Ispettore delle Legioni SS Italiane, lascio il Comando del I° Reggimento.

A tutte le Autorità Militari, Politiche e Civili, porgo il mio cameratesco saluto non disgiunto da una profonda riconoscenza per la collaborazione datami in pro di questa SS Italiana che dovrà scrivere pagine luminose per la nuova storia dell'Italia Mussoliniana.-

A NOI !

IL COMANDANTE DI REGGIMENTO
Colonnello Paolo De Maria

Colonnello Paolo De Maria's note to the Head of the Milan Province dated 24 February 1944, in which he announced how he had given up his command of the 1st Regiment to become the Inspector of the Italian SS Legions. Author's collection.

The next was formed along with most of the others in late February 1944 as Recruiting Centre VIII at Via Pietro Maestri 2, on the corner with Viale Bianca Maria. Listed as an enrolment centre on 8 April and 30 September 1944, and as an enrolment office on 7 October and 23 December 1944. Shown in an article in "Avanguardia" of 20 January 1945 as "the Recruiting Office of the Italian SS" (Ufficio Arruolamento della SS Italiana), where the "Assistence Official of the SS" (Ufficiale d'Assistenza delle SS) was located, in charge of the "SS Assistance Office" (Ufficio Assistenza SS), which provided help and support to the Italian SS soldiers and their families resident in Milan and the other provinces of Lombardy.

Officer in charge: Maggiore Giuseppe Cotta Ramusino.

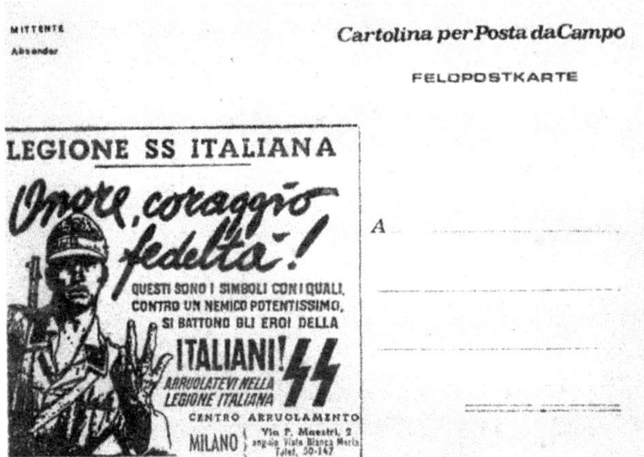

Field postcard with Boccasile's "3 fingers" design and indication of just the enrolment centre in Via Maestri in Milan. Possibly copied from an original, the paper and poor quality of this card suggest that it may be a post-war fake, or even fantasy piece.

Flyer with Boccasile's "3 fingers" but showing two recruiting offices in Milan, in Via Grossi and Via Maestri. This leaflet is believed to have been produced in early 1945.

The third was an enrolment office formed it would seem without a number at some time after July 1944, most likely in early 1945, at Via Tommaso Grossi 7.

Officer in charge: Not identified.

Ink stamp applied to books, periodicals and documents listing Milan's two enrolment offices with the "SS" as letters – a variation with the text "ARRUOLATEVI NELLA LEGIONE SS ITALIANA" ("join the Italian SS Legion", with the SS in runes) was stamped on the title page of an illustrated book about Mussolini's visit to Italian divisions training in German, 16 – 18 July 1944(7).

Il nostro onore si chiama fedeltà!

« Fedelissimi tra tutti i fedeli — ripeto — perchè non sarà forse vano chiarire che cosa voi rappresentate nel quadro di questa miracolosa riscossa della nostra Patria dopo l'infame tradimento. Voi siete quelli che non hanno avuto tentennamenti, non hanno avuto crisi di coscienza più o meno laboriose. Immediatamente, senza esitazione, voi avete sentito che non c'era altra via da seguire che quella dell'onore e vi siete schierati senz'altro a fianco dei camerati germanici, accettando totalitariamente, senza riserve alcuna, di combattere con loro per la causa comune di questa Europa, che non è solo una espressione geografica, ma si avvia a divenire una grande realtà ».

CAMERATI DELLE SS ITALIANE! Voi avete l'onore di costituire l'avanguardia delle forze europee, che realizzeranno questa nuova idea.

(dal messaggio del Maresciallo Graziani ai camerati delle SS Italiane - 30-12-1944-XXIII).

ϟϟ ϟϟ ϟϟ

ITALIANI! Voi che volete partecipare alla liberazione della Patria, alla difesa dell'Europa dall'assalto delle forze della distruzione e della negazione

ARRUOLATEVI
nella **LEGIONE SS ITALIANA**

antesignana della riscossa, figlia primogenita dell'Italia Repubblicana, sempre in linea per l'Italia, per l'Europa!

Uffici d'arruolamento:

MILANO
VIA TOMMASO GROSSI, 7 - TEL. 88-426
VIA PIETRO MAESTRI, 2 - TEL. 50-147

A 1945 flyer or poster for Milan's two enrolment offices.

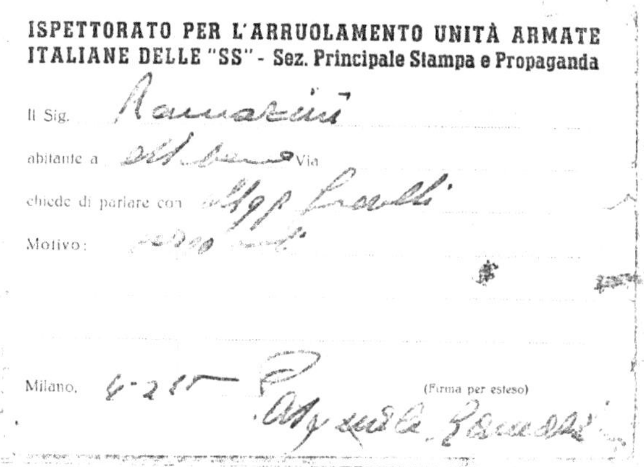

ISPETTORATO PER L'ARRUOLAMENTO UNITÀ ARMATE ITALIANE DELLE "SS" - Sez. Principale Stampa e Propaganda

Il Sig. Ramazzini

abitante a [illegible] Via

chiede di parlare con Magg. Gravelli

Motivo: [illegible]

Milano, 4-2-45 [illegible]

(Firma per esteso) [illegible]

Form used for requests to speak with a member of the Main Press and Propaganda Section of the Inspectorate for the Recruitment of Italian Armed Units ofthe SS in Milan. This one appears to be dated 4 February 1945.

By early February 1945 there was an Inspectorate for the Recruitment of Armed Italian Units of the SS (Ispettorato per l'Arruolamento Unità Armate Italiane dell "SS") in Milan, containing a number of sections, one of which was the Main Press and Propaganda Section (Sezione Principale Stampa e Propaganda). On 26 March 1945 the Deputy Chief of the Press Office, L. Muti, asked to speak with Col. Alvero Gravelli. Milan was liberated between 25 and 29 April 1945.

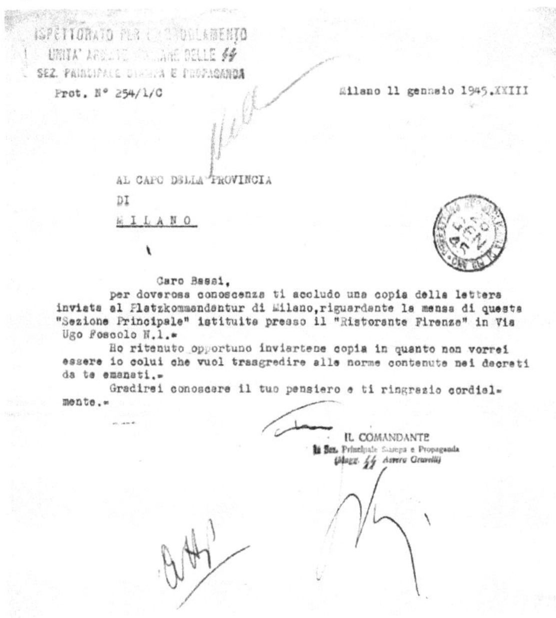

ISPETTORATO PER [illegible]OLAMENTO
UNITA' AR[illegible]ANE DELLE SS
SEZ. PRINCIPALE [illegible] E PROPAGANDA

Prot. N° 254/1/C

Milano 11 gennaio 1945.XXIII

AL CAPO DELLA PROVINCIA
DI
MILANO

Caro Bassi,

per doverosa conoscenza ti accludo una copia della lettera inviata al Platzkommandantur di Milano, riguardante la mensa di questa "Sezione Principale" istituita presso il "Ristorante Firenze" in Via Ugo Foscolo N.1.=

Ho ritenuto opportuno inviartene copia in quanto non vorrei essere io colui che vuol trasgredire alle norme contenute nei decreti da te emanati.=

Gradirei conoscere il tuo pensiero e ti ringrazio cordialmente.=

IL COMANDANTE
la Sez. Principale Stampa e Propaganda
(Magg. SS Asvero Gravelli)

Signed carbon copy of a letter dated 11 January 1945 from Magg. SS Asvero Gravelli, head of the Main Press and Propaganda Section of the Enrolment Inspectorate of the Armed Italian Units of the SS in Milan, to the Head of the Milan Province concerning his Main Section's mess at the Ristorante Firenze (Restaurant Florence) in Milan's Via Ugo Foscolo No. 1.

AI GIOVANI DELLE CLASSI 1928 e 1929

Col consenso dei vostri genitori potrete anche voi avere l'ambito onore di appartenere alla Legione **SS** Italiana.

Giovinezza d'Italia!

Ricordate! La vostra Patria è in pericolo! La vostra casa, le vostre donne possono diventare facile preda del barbaro nemico. Seguite l'impulso generoso del vostro cuore, difendete il vostro onore. Accorrete nella Legione **SS** Italiana.

Trattamento economico pari a quello delle **SS** Germaniche.

L'addestramento avviene in Italia.

Per schiarimenti ed informazioni rivolgetevi a Varese in Via Vittorio Veneto, 9 Telefono 23-79.

Flyer for volunteers born in 1928 and 1929, without specification as to whether this was for a centre or an office.

L'ora della difesa ad oltranza è suonata

GIOVENTU' D' ITALIA !

Accorri sulle balze degli Appennini per la tua battaglia

LA

LEGIONE ϟϟ ITALIANA

chiama tutti alla riscossa

Centro di Reclutamento per la Provincia di Varese
Via Vittorio Veneto, 9 - Telef. 23-79

Flyer for the Recruiting Centre for the Province of Varese.

PAVIA

Formed as a secondary enrolment centre (*centro d'arruolamento secondaria*) at the headquarters of the Republican Fascist Federation at Palazzo Broletto. Subordinate hierarchically to Cremona, it was not listed at 8 April 1944, but its existence as an enrolment centre and then office was confirmed in lists published on 30 September and 7 October 1944 respectively. Pavia was liberated on 26 April 1945.

Officer in charge: Not identified.

RODENGO-SAIANO

See under Cremona.

SONDRIO

It is possible that the Recruitment Centre/Enrolment Office of the Italian SS Volunteers Legion (*Centro di Reclutamento IX/Ufficio Arruolamento Legione Volontari S.S. italiani*) in Bergamo was transferred to Sondrio prior to the end of September 1944.

VARESE

Formed as a secondary centre at the Villa Litti in Piazza della Motta 4, but subsequently transferred to Via Vittorio Veneto 9 as an enrolment centre (*Centro d'Arruolamenti*), where it was not listed on 8 April but on 30 September 1944. Subordinate hierarchically to Milan, it was listed also as a the Recruitment Centre for the Varese Province (*Centro di Reclutamento per la Provincia di Varese*) and as an enrolmnent office on 7 October 1944. An ink stamp with the words "Italian SS Armed Units/Varese Enrolment Section (*Unità Armate Italiane SS, Sezione Arruolamento Varese*) has also been found, the only example so far encountered of the designation "Section" (*Sezione*), presumably another name for a secondary centre. Varese was liberated in late April 1945. See also Busto Arsizio.

Noi delle Legioni SS Volontari Italiani

1) Siamo italiani al cento per cento, non mercenari, non venduti a nessuno.

2) Siamo i traditi, siamo coloro che, dopo aver sostenuto su tutti i fronti l'onore del combattimento, furono lasciati in balìa del nemico.

3) Siamo coloro che nelle ore più oscure, quando un vento di follia suicida travolse animi ed intelletti, minoranze di fede, si strinsero attorno ai simboli dell'Italianità e della Alleanza.

4) Siamo i volontari della morte, decisi a lavare con il sangue l'onta del vergognoso tradimento.

5) Siamo coloro che non hanno dimenticato i gloriosi Caduti di tutte le guerre.

6) Non siamo gli arricchiti e gli arrivisti, non abbiamo mai ricoperto cariche. Vogliamo solamente che l'Italia sia grande, sempre più grande, affinchè il sacrificio dei suoi figli migliori non sia stato vano.

7) Consideriamo i nostri nemici i capitalisti, gli sfruttatori, la borghesia pacifista e tutti gli affetti da «Filia» che non sia per l'ITALIA.

8) Crediamo in Mussolini ed Hitler e nel popolo lavoratore dei campi e delle officine.

9) Siamo all'Avanguardia nella idea di giustizia, solidarietà e uguaglianza fra i popoli.

10) IL NOSTRO ONORE SI CHIAMA FEDELTÀ.

CENTRO ARRUOLAMENTI:

Via Vittorio Veneto, 9 - Varese - Telefono 23-79

Flyer for the Enrolment Centre in Varese with Boccasile's "submachine gun and dagger".

ITALIANI!

Quando ululano le sirene d'allarme correte verso i vostri rifugi!

Quando siete sulla strada e sentite i cacciabombardieri, riparate al coperto! I "liberatori" anglo-americani avrebbero diversamente troppo piacere di liberarvi della vita.

Non passa un giorno che non ci porti nuove segnalazioni delle loro azioni infami e vili. Essi si divertono, adoperando le loro armi di bordo per far la caccia sugli inermi civili: colle armi di bordo essi tirano su donne e bambini, come se fossero delle lepri.

Anche nella Italia occupata da questi "liberatori" i nostri connazionali vengono trattati come selvaggina. La non sparano colle armi di bordo da una data altezza sui passanti; ma rubano ai nostri fratelli tutti i viveri e saccheggiano le case che non sono state ancora distrutte dai loro attacchi terroristici.

L'orrore per tali barbari sistemi di guerra si unisce all'incredulità che uomini in veste di combattenti possano scendere a tanta bassezza, a tanto sadismo. Ma forse per questi aviatori usciti dalle bande di "gangster" o dalle carceri americane, gli Italiani non sono considerate creature di Dio, ma semplicemente oggetti per esercitarsi in una caccia morbosamente emozionante.

L'orrore attanaglia il cuore, l'incredulità la mente, ma purtroppo questa è la realtà. E così si parla di questi mostri umani, si commentano e si condannano le loro nefande gesta, si malediscono i loro delitti.

Ma che vale la parola e la verbale protesta senza azione? Nulla.

È giunto il tempo di muoversi, di agire, di reagire, di difendersi, poichè si tratta di una lotta per la vita o per la morte.

Due sono i sistemi per opporsi a tanto inumano nemico: l'uno è quello di lavorare, lavorare senza tregua per rafforzare la difesa della Patria e creare le premesse di un ritorno offensivo; l'altro è quello di vestire la gloriosa uniforme militare, per tornare al combattimento, il quale, se sorretto da estrema decisione e da fede incrollabile, con l'aiuto dell'invitta ed invincibile Germania, ci riporterà al successo ed alla cacciata dei barbari profanatori del nostro sacro suolo, degli assassini delle nostre donne e dei nostri figli.

Z II/146

Ink stamp for the enrolment section in Varese on an undated propaganda leaflet printed by the German Propaganda Detachment (Propaganda-Staffel) with reference II/146.

MARSHES, THE (LE MARCHE)

ANCONA

Formed as Recruiting Centre XIX at the German garrison command headquarters (*Ortskommandantur*). Hierarchically subordinate to Bologna, it was listed as an enrolment centre on 8 April 1944, but was absent from lists published on 30 September and 7 October 1944. Ancona was liberated on 18/19 July 1944.

Officer in charge: *Maggiore* Rinaldo Grattini.

MACERATA

Formed as Recruiting Centre XX at the Fascist Party headquarters (*Casa del Fascio*) at Via L. Rossi 26. Hierarchically subordinate to Bologna, it was listed as an enrolment centre on 8 April 1944. Macerata was liberated on 30 June 1944.

Officer in charge: *Sottotenente* Attilio Gelli.

PESARO

Formed as a Recruiting Centre at the headquarters of the Republican Fascist Federation in Viale Palestro and hierarchically a secondary centre under Bologna, it was not included in a list published on 8 April 1944. Pesaro was liberated on 2 September 1944.

Officer in charge: Not identified.

PIEDMONT (PIEMONTE)

ALESSANDRIA

Formed as Recruiting Centre IV in room 18 of the Albergo (hotel) "Italia" and operational from 1 March 1944 at Via Modena 5 and finally Via Mazzoni 9 and 11, where it was still reported at 23 December 1944. Hierarchically subordinate to Milan, it was listed as an enrolment centre on 8 April and 30 September, and an enrolment office on 7 October 1944. Alessandria was liberated on 29 April 1945.

Officer in charge: *Capitano* Umberto Uboldi.

AOSTA

Formed as Recruiting Centre V in Palazzo Littorio. Subordinate hierarchically to Milan and listed as an enrolment centre on 8 Aporil 1944, it was absent from lists dated 30 September and 7 October 1944. A newspaper advertisement of unknown date gave the Recruiting Centre in Turin as also being responsible for the provinces of Aosta and Cuneo. Aosta was liberated on 28 April 1945.

Officer in charge: *Sottotenente* Giuseppe Tavano.

CUNEO

Formed as Recruiting Centre II at the Vittorio Emanuele II army barracks, but subsequently transferred to the head office of a local bank (Palazzo della Cassa di Risparmio) at Via Roma 15. It was hierarchically subordinate to Milan. A leaflet published by the Istituto Poligrafico "Imperiale" of Mondovì referred to the "Recruiting District"

(*Distretto di arruolamento*) of Cuneo. A newspaper advertisement of unknown date gave the Recruiting Centre in Turin as also being responsible for the provinces of Cuneo and Aosta. Listed as an enrolment centre on 8 April 1945, but not on 30 September and 7 October 1944. Cuneo was liberated on 28 April 1945.

Officer in charge: *Sottotenente* Pietro Careri.

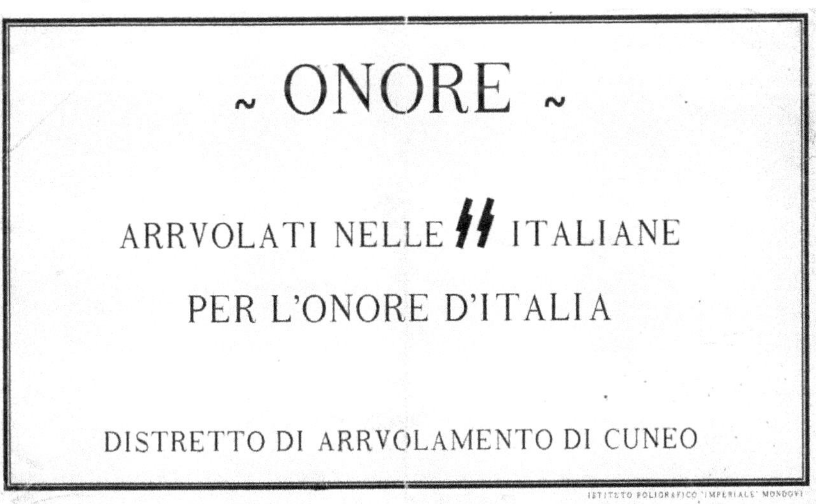

Flyer for the Cuneo Recruiting District of the Italian SS printed in Mondovi.

Poster &/or flyer for the Enrolment Centre in Novara, which also covered the province of Vercelli (Corbatti/Nava).

NOVARA

Formed as Recruiting Centre VI and in March 1944 given as also being responsible for recruitment in the province of Vercelli. Originally located at Via Liceo Carlo Alberto 2[(8)], but subsequently transferred to Corso Gabriele D'Annunzio 25 at the corner with Via Silvio Pellico. Listed as aan enrolment centre on 8 April and 30 September, it was shown as an enrolment office on 7 October and 23 December 1944. The German forces surrendered in Novara on 26 April 1945.

Officer in charge: *Tenente* Leonardo Caputo, although *Tenente Colonello* A. Negri has also been found at the Recruitment Center (*Werbestelle* Novara) in Corso Gabriele D'Annunzio 25.

TURIN (TORINO)

Formed as Recruiting Centre III on the 2nd floor of Via Arcivescovado 2, on the corner with Via Roma. Hierarcically subordinate to Milan, it was absent from a list of enrolment centres dated 8 April, but was subsequently listed as an enrolment centre and an enrolment office on 30 September and 7 October 1944 respectively. It was confirmed as an office on 23 December 1944. An undated newspaper announcement with Boccasile's "3 fingers" artwork showed this as an enrolment centre for not only the province of Turin, but also those of Aosta and Cuneo. Turin was liberated on 25/30 April 1945.

Officer in charge: *Capitano* Arrigo Zanotti.

Boccasile's "3 fingers" in an announcement calling for volunteers to join the Italian SS Legion published by the Recruitment Centre for Turin, Cuneo and Aosta.

TUSCANY (TOSCANA)

APUANIA MASSA (today Massa Carrara)

Formed as Recruitment Centre XXVI at Villa Grossi in Viale Litoraneo 38, but subsequently transferred to the 3rd floor of Piazza Farini 1. Hierarchically subordinate to Florence, it was listed as an enrolment centre on 8 April 1944 but was not in lists published on 30 September and 7 October 1944. Apuania was liberated on 10/11 April 1945.

Officer in charge: Originally *Capitano* Beppino Chiappini, but who took over after he was captured and shot by partisans at Camporaghena di Comano on 15 November 1944 is not known

FLORENCE (FIRENZE, FLORENZ)

Formed as Recruiting Centre XVII on the first floor of Via Fiume 14. Hierarchically subordinate to Cremona, it was in its turn responsible for the centres in Apuania, Grosseto, Perugia, Pisa, Siena and Viterbo. It was listed as an enrolment centre on 8 April 1944. Florence was liberated between 4 August and 2 September 1944.

Officer in charge: *Capitano/Waffen-Hauptsturmführer* Leale Martelli.

SS Cosa vuol dire LEGIONI VOLONTARI SS ITALIANI?

Vuol dire essere VOLONTARIO fra i volontari, ARDITO fra gli arditi.

Essere nelle SS significa FEDELTA' e dedizione alla PATRIA, se occorre fino al sacrificio.

Formidabilmente armati con le più moderne armi germaniche, perfettamente addestrati ed equipaggiati, al fianco dei camerati germanici le nostre Legioni SS sapranno rinnovare le gesta eroiche dei combattenti italiani.

Sarà accettato chiunque si presenta, purchè abbia animo di ITALIANO e fermamente voglia COMBATTERE.

Le domande si ricevono presso il ***Centro di reclutamento in Firenze Via Fiume n. 14 piano primo*** a cui gli interessati potranno rivolgersi per ogni informazione e schiarimento.

Per la Provincia di Pistoia gli interessati potranno rivolgersi al Centro di arruolamento della Federazione dei Fasci Repubblicani via S. Andrea.

Recruiting leaflet inviting volunteers to attend at the Recruiting Centres on the first floor of Florence's Via Fiume 14 or that at the Federation of Republican Fasces in Pistoia's Via S. Andrea. Note the Republican fasces and primitive attempt at the Siegrunen.

GROSSETO

Formed as Recruiting Centre XXIII at the headquarters of the Republican Fascist Federation in Via Saffi, but subsequently transferred, first to Villa Pallini in Via Lanza and then to the second floor of Corso Carlo Alberto 85. Hierarchically subordinate to Florence, it was listed as an enrolment centre on 8 April 1944. Grosseto was liberated on 16 June 1944.

Officer in charge: *Tenente* Antonio Marino.

PISA

Formed as Recruiting Centre XXV at the headquarters of the Republican Fascist Federation in the Palazzo del Littorio at Via XXIX Maggio 41, but it subsequently followed the Federation in being transferred to Via San Martino 1 in March 1944. Hierarchically subordinate to Florence, it was listed as an enrolment centre on 8 April 1944. Pisa was liberated on 2 September 1944.

Officer in charge: *Tenente* Giacomo Lombardo.

PISTOIA

Although not listed in 1944, an unnumbered enrolment centre was located in the offices of the Federarion of Republican Fasces in Via S. Andrea, Pistoia.

See Firenze for a recruiting leaflet for the provinces of both Florence and Pistoia.

Poster for the enrolment office for the Italian SS Legion in Padua.

SIENA

Formed as Recruiting Centre XXIV in the offices of the National After Work Organization (*Opera Nazionale Dopolavoro*, or O.N.D. – the Fascist equivalent of the Nazi "Strength Through Joy" organization - *Kraft durch Freude*, or KdF) in Piazza Unità Italiana. It was listed as an enrolment centre on 8 April 1944. Siena was liberated on 3 July 1944.

Officer in charge: *Capitano* Filippo Gentiletti.

UMBRIA

PERUGIA

Formed as Enrolment Centre XXI in room 52 of the Albergo (hotel) "Brufani", but transferred by March 1944 to Largo Vannucci 11. Hierarchically subordinate to Florence, it was listed as an enrolment centre on 8 April 1944. Perugia was liberated on 20 June 1944. Officer in charge: *Capitano* Giulio Carignola.

VENETO

PADUA (PADOVA)

Formed as Recruting Centre XIV at Via Galileo Galilei 22, but subsequently transferred to Piazza Cavour 10. Subordinate hierarchically to Verona, it was listed as an enrolment centre on 8 April 1944, but was absent from other lists so far found for the remainder of that year but was shown as an enrolment office for the Italian Volunteer SS Legione (*Ufficio Arruolamento delle Legioni Volontari SS Italiani*) in an undated poster. In the first days of October 1944 *Tenente SS* Vasco Mingori was sent from the recruiting centre in Venice to the "Sub-Section" (*Sottosezione*) in Padua[9]. On his way by car he was stopped by partisans between Mestre and Padua and taken to their headquarters, but some days later was handed over to another group of partisans who, fearing the approach of the enemy, killed him on 13 or 14 October. Padua was liberated on 27 April 1945.

Officer in charge: *Sottotenente* Mario Tarantino.

TREVISO

Formed as Recruiting Centre XIII at Rivale Castelvecchio 4, but subsequently transferred, first to Via S. Margherita 27 and then to Vicolo Nino Bixio 2. Subordinate to Verona, it was listed as an enrolment centre on 8 April and 30 September 1944 and an enrolment office on 7 October 1944. As at 23 December 1944 it was reported to have been at the headquarters of the Republican Fascist Federation, but it is not known whether this was at

Vicolo Nino Bixio 2 or elsewhere in the town. Allied troops arrived in Treviso on 29 April 1945. Officer in charge: *Sottotenente* Rinaldo Poiano.

Undated leaflet printed in Venice for the enrolment offices of both Treviso and Venice.

VENICE (VENEZIA, VENEDIG)

Formed as an unnumbered secondary centre in the offices of the Assicurazioni Generali, then and now Italy's leading insurance company, in the Palazzo Assicurazioni (insurance building) at Piazza San Marco 105. Subordinate hierarchically to Verona, it was not listed on 8 April, but was on lists dated 30 September and then 7 October 1944, as an enrolment centre and then office respectively, the latter title confirmed on 23 December 1944. Venice was liberated in late April 1945. Officer in charge: Not identified.

VERONA

Formed as Recruiting Centre XI on the 2nd floor of Via Ponte Rafiolo 4, but subsequently transferred in March 1944 to Via Mazzini 80. Subordinated hierarchically to Cremona, it conrtrolled in its turn Bolzano, Padua, Treviso, Udine and Venice. Confirmed as a centre on 8 April and 30 September and as an office on 7 October 1944, it was still at Via Mazzini 80 on 23 December 1944. Verona was liberated on 24/25 April 1945. Officer in charge *Maggiore* Giovanni Zocchi.

THE GERMAN-CONTROLLED OPERATIONAL ZONES

"Pre-Alps" Operations Zone (Zona d'Operazioni Prealpi, Operationszone Alpenvorland – OZAV) – today Trentino Alto Adige

The German-speaking part of northern Italy, known today as the South Tyrol (Alto Adige in Italian and Südtirol in German). The majority of men served in various elements of the *Waffen-SS*, in particular the *24. Waffen-Gebirgs-(Karstjäger) Division der SS*, not the Italian SS, as well as in local security forces, such as the S.O.D. in Bolzano and the C.S.T. in Trento, but a recruiting centre (*Werbestelle*) was established in Bolzano for the *Milizia Armata – Waffen Miliz.*

BOLZANO (BOZEN)

Formed as Recruitment Centre XXIX in Room 81 at the Stadt Hotel in the provincial capital by 25 March 1944, but transferred elsewhere before the end of that month. Although authorized and hierarchically subordinate to Verona, this Office never became operational. Bolzano was liberated on 25 April 1945. Officer in charge: *Capitano* Ciro Perugini.

UDINE

The Recruitment Centre for the *24. Waffen-Gebirgs- (Kartsjäger) Division der SS* was in Udine and it is possible that it also provided men for the Italian SS Legion, however it was not given a Roman numeral as were the others in February/March 1944 and no such centre has been found listed specifically for the Italian SS(10).

"Adriatic Litoral" Operations Zone (Zona d'Operazioni Litorale Adriatico, Operationszone Adriatisches Küstenland – OZAK) – today Friuli Venezia Giulia

No centre was set up in the capital of the OZAK, Trieste, presumably because all volunteers in that city and area were sent to the "*Karstjäger*" formation, the local Civic Guard, or German formations.

Note

(1) Boccasile was born in 1901 in Bari and enjoyed considerable popularity and success as an illustrator before the war, specializing in advertising posters and magazine covers, often depicting voluptuous and scantily-dressed young women. He joined the Italian SS and by mid-March 1945 held the position of *Sonderführer* (Z), that is a specialist officer with a rank equivalent to that of a *Leutnant* (*Waffen-Untersturmführer*) or *Oberleutnant* (*Waffen-Obersturmführer*). At that date he was a member of the Press and Propaganda Department (*Abteilung Press und Propaganda*) in the Italian Armed Formations of the SS. Boccasile survived the war and continued to work as an artist. He died in Milan in 1952.

(2) Shown without a number on the Personnel Office's map. See text.

(3) Lazzero: "*Le SS Italiane. Storia dei 20.000 che giurarono fedeltà a Hitler*", page 61.

(4) By including Cremona, Youngs thus did not include Bolzano in his total of 29, suggesting his source was Lazzero – see Bibliography.

(5) Shown as Lino in original document.

(6) Shown incorrectly as Corso Zanarselli 36, when listed as a Centre for the Unità Armate Italiane delle *SS Italienische Waffenverbände der SS*.

(7) "*Il Duce tra i Soldati dell'Italia Fascista Repubblicana*".

(8) At June 1944: Legione Volontari Italiani, Uff. Arruolamento di Novara, Via Liceo Carlo Alberto 2.

(9) Youngs listed Padua as a primary centre.

(10) Lazzero, p. 61, however, lists it as hierarchically subordinate to Verona.

Bibliography

Corbatti, Sergio & Nava, Marco (pseud.): "*Sentire – Pensare – Volere: Storia della Legione SS Italiana*", Ritter S.a.s., Milan, 2001

"*Duce tra i Soldati dell'Italia Repubblicana, Il*", Edizioni "Erre", Venezia – Milano, 1944-XXII

Lazzero, Ricciotti" "*Le SS italiane. Storia dei 20.000 che giurarono fedeltà a Hitler*", Rizzoli Editore

Morini, F.: "*Parma nella Repubblica Sociale*", Edizioni La Sfinge, Parma. 1989

Novarese, Dr. Marco: "*La Legione SS Italiana*", in "Storia del XX Secolo", N. 31, December 1997.

TITOLI PUBBLICATI - ALREADY PUBLISHING

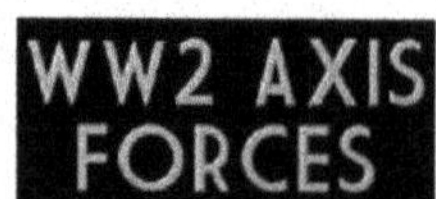
WW2 AXIS
FORCES

www.Ingramcontent.com/pod-product-compliance
Ingram Content Group UK Ltd.
Pitfield, Milton Keynes, MK11 3LW, UK
UKHW061702190726
13853UKWH00008B/2352